Gerard Hoffnung

Gerard

his biography by

ANNETTA HOFFNUNG

with a foreword by

PETER USTINOV

AURUM PRESS

Paperback edition published 1994 by Aurum Press Limited, 25 Bedford Avenue, London WC1B 3AT
First published 1988 by Gordon Fraser Gallery Limited, London and Bedford

A catalogue record for this book is available from the British Library.

ISBN 1 85410 288 5

Typeset in Monophoto Apollo by August Filmsetting, Haydock, St Helens
Printed in Singapore
Designed by Sarah Menon

To Benedict, Emily and Martha

ACKNOWLEDGEMENTS

I would like to offer my thanks for the kindness of a number of individuals who have assisted me in the preparation of this book. I must make special mention of Anni Herrmann, Ann Gould and Morag Morris, without whose generous advice and encouragement I doubt that this volume would have been completed. I also acknowledge gratefully the valuable assistance of Tom Bergman and Sir George Engle QC, both of whom gave generously of their time and expertise. Many friends have let me quote from *O Rare Hoffnung*, Sybil Shaw, Jean Atkinson, and Ian Messiter have allowed me to publish letters, Linda MacGregor has made available material for me to use, and Rowland Emett, Henri Henrion, David de Groot, Sam Wanamaker, Antony Wilson and the Headmaster of Highgate School have lent me original drawings. I am deeply indebted to all of them. The photographs of my family and the majority of those relating to the Hoffnung Music Festival were taken by Rob Melville.

I acknowledge the courtesy of Souvenir Press for kindly allowing the reproduction of the following drawings: three from *Hoffnung's Little Ones*; one from *The Maestro*; eight from *The Hoffnung Symphony Orchestra*; eight from *Hoffnung in Harmony* and one from *Hoffnung's Acoustics;* the proprietors of *Punch* for allowing me to reproduce drawings published in their magazine; *The New Statesman* for use of a cartoon by Vicky and for allowing me to publish a letter from David Low; Guinness plc for two drawings and two poems by Stanley Penn; Scolar Press for six drawings from *The Isle of Cats*; *The Irish Times, The Guardian, The Scotsman, Yorkshire Post, Daily Mail, The Times,* EMI Ltd and *Connoisseur* for permitting me to use extracts from their publications; BBC Enterprises for allowing me to use two photographs of broadcasts; Oelrich Advertising Ltd for the use of a cartoon from an advertisement for Lockwood & Carlisle Ltd; Esso and Ford Motor Company for their permission to use drawings from past promotions and The Open University for permission to use an extract from their pamphlet. My thanks are also due to the following for allowing me to print two copyright poems: Trustees of the John Betjeman Estate for 'The Lift' published in *John Betjeman's Uncollected Poems* by John Murray, and Associated Book Publishers for 'Do Bishops Brood?' by Percy Cudlipp.

Occasionally I have endeavoured, unsuccessfully, to trace people, or sometimes have not even known whom to seek out. In these few cases I have gone ahead and published material, trusting that I will not be held culpable. I owe a great deal to those friends and strangers, who have shared with me reminiscences of Gerard.

Finally I would like to place on record my gratitude to the staff of Gordon Fraser for their patience, warm enthusiasm and the feeling I have been given all along that they want this book to be every bit as good as I do.

FOREWORD

I never met Gerard Hoffnung, but that does not mean I do not know him, and know him well. Despite his tragically early death, his circle of acquaintances is still growing to this day, for a very valid reason. He conducts a very public love affair with music.

His satirical drawings are in a great German tradition, and he has affinities with both Wilhelm Busch, the creator of Max and Moritz, and with Zille, the wonderful recorder of the pre-1914 Berlin scene, but both these artists possess at times a quietly savage *gemutlichkeit* with explicit criticism of social values when applied to domestic life. As a consequence, they are both deliciously inseparable from the times they lived in. Hoffnung knows no such strictures.

Man's eternal struggle with harp and winds, timpani and brass and strings, are recorded in all their extravagance, and every possibility of indignity is superbly exploited. There is no limit of time or of place to these practices and malpractices. Every generation of musicians renews the age old struggle for ascendancy over the instruments of their choice, and luckily Hoffnung was there to record their perplexities and sometimes bitter victories for all time.

He does not even spare the most pretentious of the breed – those who produce no sounds themselves apart from grunts and weird abstract utterances which are but the emotional overflow of their choreography – the conductors, those who receive the congratulations and who generously invite the orchestra to rise in order to share in the applause. Victories are usually attributed to generals, a few medals to the men.

Hoffnung's filigree work on the architecture of music is never there to mock or to deride, but rather as a commitment. It is quite evident that this genius, at times gentle and poetic, at others preposterous and jolly, is ever in the service of the art. It is just that Hoffnung's devotion to and understanding of music expresses itself in a way that was natural to him, much as the juggler in the sentimental medieval tale juggled before the effigy of Our Lady as his contribution towards the art of piety.

The greatest compliment of Hoffnung's superficial irreverence, which is merely the outer expression of a deep and noble reverence, comes from the musicians themselves. They are his most faithful audience. And then, for such a fellow, what better name than Hoffnung, the German word for hope.

PETER USTINOV

July 1988   London

PREFACE

On several occasions Gerard announced that he felt he had not long to live. 'I shall die young you know,' he would tell me quite seriously. How strange that I never took him up on this. What prompted this feeling? What was going on?

Of course one reason the conversation never progressed was that the prospect affected me so deeply I could not bear to contemplate it. Once when I protested at this appalling prediction he said comfortingly, 'Remember there will always be music and paintings and many good friends'. I found this small comfort. Neither could I really believe that he was serious, nor that this larger-than-life, exuberant man with so much vitality and energy had any true presentiment of an early death. Sadly, his premonition was to be borne out by events.

One morning I was downstairs with the children seeing to last-minute preparations for lunch, when I heard him call. Sensing urgency in his voice I ran upstairs to his study and found him collapsed upon his sofa. I was in time to be with him for his brief remaining moments of consciousness. He died in hospital some two hours later from a cerebral haemorrhage. It was 28 September 1959 and he was thirty-four years old.

My children provided a reason for keeping sane. Gerard was right, too, about friends for they were legion. They, also, were heart-broken. They shared my grief and enacted untold kindnesses. Many years later I started working on this book during spare moments. The collecting and collating of material, most of it at hand, was straightforward, but there remained the daunting and, to me, formidable task of conveying a picture of someone as mercurial as Gerard. The twenty-first and twenty-fifth anniversaries of his death came and went and now it is the twenty-ninth – not a neat round figure to commemorate, but then Gerard was not a conformist either.

That he was a rare human being is certainly true. As a friend once
remarked, God was kind to him and saw to it that his qualities and
his gifts were endearing ones. They were there, too, from the very
start, and he displayed them constantly for all the world to see. They
remained unchanged whatever the circumstances he encountered
and difficulties he experienced. His secret, I am convinced, was his
enormous humanity and warmth; after all, only these qualities can
arouse reciprocal feelings of trust, enthusiasm and laughter. In our
marriage, these qualities abounded, to the extent that I felt a sense of
wonder at being part of this quite exceptional life. Perhaps his great
humanity, so much reflected in his work, explains Gerard's success
in his lifetime and the high regard in which he is held today by so
many people who never knew him.

In Berlin on 22 March 1925, a baby boy, Gerhardt, was born into a prosperous German-Jewish family. His father, Ludwig Hoffnung, was a business man, a well-to-do grain merchant. He was inclined to be gruff and did not suffer fools gladly.

Gerard's mother, Hilde, on the other hand, was a woman of great sensitivity. She was a pianist of considerable ability and enjoyed painting and drawing. Her early sketchbooks that have survived show a sense of humour and keen observation and her drawings give an indication of her personality. Some of the drawings have an affinity with Gerard's childhood illustrations. She must have been more than encouraging in her attitude towards his early enjoyment of and absorption in drawing. Her childhood was spent in Berlin with her parents and younger sister, Ilse.

A sketch by Gerard's mother, Hilde, of her sister Ilse.

Hilde studied music and, shortly before the First World War, married a fellow student, a young man with the musically evocative name of Schnabel. Within the year he was killed at the Front. After four years of widowhood, Hilde Schnabel married Ludwig Hoffnung. Seven years later Gerard, a longed-for and much wanted child, was born.

Gerard's grandparents with their children, Hilde (*right*) and Ilse (*left*).

The family lived in the fashionable and exclusive district of Grunewald in a large house with a garden going down to a lake. Summer holidays were spent in Westerland and winter in St Moritz.

Hilde was a loving and adoring mother, keen to share her love of music with her son, who by the age of five was learning to play the violin. But lessons were not an immediate success, and her fond hope that they would make music together remained unfulfilled. Nevertheless, there is no doubt that it was largely due to his mother that music was soon to become such a vital part of Gerard's life. She spent endless hours playing to him, and as an adult he remembered her playing the full piano-score of most of the popular operas to him, singing all the parts. The handsomely-bound scores line my sitting-room walls today. Gerard's prodigious musical memory, which he enjoyed for the whole of his life, must have developed during that period.

Gerard with his devoted mother.

(*Below*) In his pram aged one year, and at the age of two and a half with his father in Venice.

Gerard playing in the garden in Grunewald.

Gerard at five years.

Where her son was concerned, Hilde's generosity with her time knew no bounds. As well as singing and playing the piano, they also read together fairy tales (those of the Brothers Grimm were special favourites), the heroic sagas and children's stories of his time. She found him an avid listener and she soon came to observe his passion for drawing. He filled sketchbook after sketchbook with innumerable drawings, almost as if he could not keep pace with the vividness of his imagination. Even at that very early age she must have recognised his talent. Well over a thousand of these early drawings exist today and were not abandoned even when the family had to leave Berlin and later, Italy. It tells me much of her feeling towards, and her interest and involvement with, her son.

The macabre held a gruesome fascination for him then, and throughout his lifetime. There is no doubt that while some of Gerard's early drawings are nightmarish and sinister, a few of them are barbaric in the graphic tradition of German folklore and nineteenth-century comic caricature, thus revealing his familiarity with a wide range of illustrated books.

George Engle, a good friend, writing on the subject comments:
*Altogether a strange and rather disquieting body of work to come from a
boy not yet in his teens. Curiously, however, at the age of about thirteen
Hoffnung stopped producing what I may call horrifying drawings; and
in the course of the next few years, his attitude towards horror changed
completely. As a child the creatures conjured up by his restless imagination were obviously all too real to him. With a few exceptions, they are
drawn with a seriousness that is perhaps the most frightening thing
about them. But as he grew up, Hoffnung's sense of humour intervened
between himself and his macabre imaginings, so that in due course he
came to regard the horrific in literature and in films as enormously
funny. Witness, for example, the magnificent panorama of nightmare
creatures which apeared in* Lilliput *in 1946. There is everything in this,
from Brueghel's Hell-mouth, via a whole family of middle-class
vampires, to Melies' skeleton horse. But the chuckle has ousted the
shiver.*

Drawn at the age of nine years.

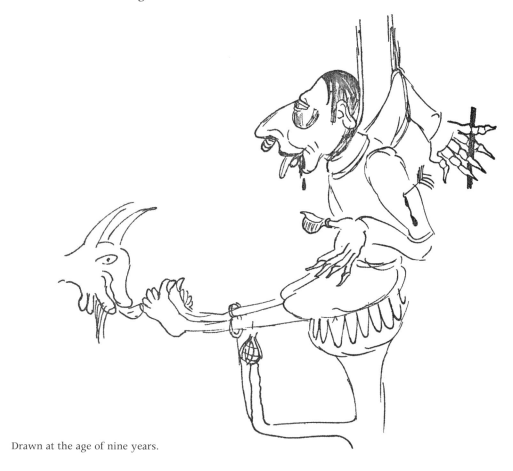

Drawn at the age of nine years.

Drawn at the age of seventeen years.

Die Gespenster.

G. Hoffnung

Illustrations to fairy tales and legends abound in his early draw-ings. An uncle of Gerard's by marriage, Bruno Adler, was teacher of art at a school Gerard attended in his early teens. He wrote about Gerard at this stage:

What particularly attracted him in the world of fairy tales was not just the macabre element, but the whole conception of fantasy. Everything that was out of the ordinary – ghosts or angels, madmen or fairies – fascinated him. He was just as responsive to a beautiful face as to an outstandingly ugly one, with the difference that he never felt impelled to reproduce the beautiful. Inspiration lay for him on the borderline of fantasy, where the unpleasant can strike one as amusing and the myster-ious looks almost homely.

Drawn at the age of twelve years.

Drawn at the age of twelve years.

Drawn at the age of eleven years.

Many of his drawings deal with humorous situations. Some have a musical theme.Others show that before he was seven he was already familiar with many of the bible stories. Had I known my mother-in-law I could have asked her how it was that a small Jewish boy with a non-religious upbringing became knowledgeable about the New Testament, Jesus Christ and the Crucifixion. His early childhood drawings of Jesus, benign, omniscient, omnipotent and beatific, have immense charm and show a deep underlying affection for the subject. This makes the humour, not normally associated with these stories, acceptable and endearing.

Drawn at the age of seven years.

Drawn at the age of twelve years.

Drawn at the age of ten years.

Drawn at the age of eleven years.

Drawn at the age of twelve years.

Drawn at the age of six years.

Drawn at the age of seven years.

(*Above and below*) Biblical illustrations drawn at the age of seven years.

Gerard did not have the patience to learn to play any musical instrument. Although a reluctant pupil of the violin, his other musical enthusiasms were nevertheless given a free rein. Two photographs bear witness to his experiments on saxophone and trumpet and, naturally enough, he had a set of drums.

Gerard with trumpet (*above*) and saxophone (*below*).

(An old friend of the family told me recently that when he first visited the Hoffnungs later on in London, a large set of jazz drums filled a corner of the room. Along with the drawings, they too had made the journey to this country.)

Angelica Caro, a school-friend and then a child of ten, describes a visit she made one afternoon to Gerard aged twelve:

Unfortunately his talents were many and the time-schedule according to which he would pursue his various passions could never be glimpsed in advance. When I arrived at his home he no longer existed for me in any of his formerly known guises, but had committed himself body and soul to his music. Between hitting a cymbal and blowing a horn, 'My jazz band,' he explained; this was rather unnecessary since the spectacle spoke for itself. Loki (his nickname at the time) did not just own a jazz band, he was the band. Enthroned among his countless instruments, he handled them with dizzying dexterity, tossing his head and thumping his feet, his face red and his eyes almost popping out with the effort of being in time with whatever infernal melody was cruising about in his head. When I left his house about an hour or so later, we hadn't spoken more than a few dozen words and I am sure he was completely unaware of my exit.

Gerard with André Previn.

A photograph of Gerard was taken in 1936 with the young André Previn when the two families met holidaying in Kornov. His mother describes in a letter how Gerard put on his own show during the children's festivities there, coaching a fat boy to be his stooge and performing on the stage to the delight of nearly a hundred children. She ends:

As a finale, with André at the piano and Gerard clowning on the drums etc., the children just couldn't stop laughing and the band was delighted with the performance.

This might be considered as motherly adulation, but knowing Gerard's ability to convulse his audiences in later years I can believe that it was a foretaste of many future occasions when he had his public rolling in the aisles.

Gerard's mother was not the only person to be surprised and often delighted by her son's antics and performances; the impressions of people I have met who knew him at that time have been equally vivid. Vera Lachmann, headmistress of his school in Berlin, whom I met after Gerard's death wrote:

There was once an unforgettable performance of Gerd's in the school garden. His part was Loki, god of fire, the trickster, the wily one. Right from the first rehearsal he was amazing. He did not recite the role, but veritably transformed himself into a fickle, dancing, teasing flame, bounding over the stage in pantomimic ecstasy, with outbursts of impish laughter. From that day on his nick-name in the school was Loki and under that name he will be remembered by his classmates and teachers. . . .

Gerard aged six years.

By the time Gerard was seven years of age, Hitler had come to power in Germany and a free choice of education had become impossible. He was enrolled in a school for young Jewish children where, from the age of ten, his school reports show not only a lack of application but also a tendency to amuse his fellow-pupils at the expense of his teachers – and, as it then seemed, of his education in general. His headmistress reported in 1936:

. . .If you really want to stay in our school you will have to change completely. Your grimacing and grinning is intolerable. . . . for once remember to bring your books, writing materials and exercise books to school with you.

And in 1937 came her remarks:

. . . Stop this fooling which you should have grown out of by now, so that we can all take you more seriously. Croaking and squeaking are not funny, just dreadful. If ever I see your face natural and serious and composed, I sigh with relief. Do you think your constant clowning endears you to anyone? We are fed up with your face-pulling. You have improved a little. Please, please make an effort.

Ironically, this small Jewish school was situated next door to Himmler's house. This was a large building, under constant guard by carefully chosen members of the SS. On one occasion, when some of the boys were playing in the school yard, their ball inadvertently

Private Unterrichts-Gemeinschaft Jagowstraße

Jüdische Privatschule
von Dr. Vera Lachmann
BERLIN - GRUNEWALD
Jagowstr. 35

Zeugnis *Winter* -Halbjahr 19*36/37*

für *Gerd Hoffnung*

bounced over the wall into Himmler's garden. It was Gerard, undeterred, who asked one of the SS guards for it back – a request that was curtly refused. Yet the appeal succeeded for the guard, on going off duty, threw the ball back into the school yard.

I know of no stories, anecdotes or records that show any personal catastrophic effect of the Nazi regime on the Hoffnung family. No doubt Gerard's schooling would have been different had the political structure remained normal and it is true that the sensitivity and imagination that made Gerard an easily frightened child could not have been helped in any way by the political climate. The sudden emigration and the eventual splitting-up of the family were the inevitable consequence of the threatening situation.

Drawn at the age of thirteen years.

From a letter written by his mother to her sister, Ilse, in 1937 we learn that his parents were clearly worried about their son and had sought advice.

Yesterday Gerard played his violin at a concert at the school festival. He was the only soloist and won a lot of applause. It may interest you to hear what a paediatrician and two graphologists have commented. They say, judging from his drawings (from five years onwards), my descriptions, and their observations and talks with Gerard, that his reactions are healthy and normal. He is enormously gifted artistically, but not only for drawing which both graphologists see as an expression of great imagination which is of 100 per cent importance. His drawing is the medium through which he channels his imaginative graphic skills and powers of imagination. His absent-mindedness and lack of mental disci-
pline, as well as the other negative traits in his character, are the

Drawn at the age of seven years.

normal consequence of such a gifted person.
After all, there must be some weaknesses
somewhere, some of which cannot be
changed and others which will improve
with time as he grows older. But never
should such a child be sent to boarding
school as one cannot expect teachers or
pupils to treat such a child with the same
care as a sensible mother. . . . The boy is
frightened because, through his imagin-
ation he is drawn to everything that is
sensational, thereby he himself intensi-
fies the anxiety (which to a greater or
lesser extent, is felt by everybody) till in
the end he is scared by his own grimaces.
This is a vicious circle, it is obvious that
the boy cannot exhaust his vivid imagin-

ation on a stone, a flower or a postage stamp, but instead is drawn to
everything which is in any way sensational, bloodcurdling or otherwise
exceptional.

Despite this parental concern, there was always the lighter side of
life and in 1937 Gerard had the lead in a play:
The mask he made couldn't have been bettered. . . . Hair, painted beard
and eyebrows he had made from an old fur of mine, the nose was sharp-
ly pointed by chalk lines. He draws all the time, but his music doesn't
suffer, only us. He says he is a member of a detective club and is covered
with tattoos which I would have thought had more to do with criminals,
but is really an excuse not to wash.

Regardless of anxieties about Gerard, the Hoffnungs continued to
enjoy their music and in 1937 Gerard was taken to his first opera –
Die Meistersinger. On his return from the theatre he sat down and

Gerard's version of
Act II: *Die Meistersinger*. Drawn at the age
of twelve years.

Now at last, I have found happiness *

* They pay me 10 Mark the hour.

drew a cartoon of the fighting scene at the end of Act II. We know that he made a second drawing (unfortunately lost) for his grandmother describes it thus in a letter:

Gerd recently made a beautiful drawing – the Beckmesser scene from Meistersinger. . . . Nothing was forgotten. The lilac trees, the shoe in front of Hans Sach's door, every detail of the roof-tops, the bench with the loving couple, the neighbours looking out of the windows: also the heads of the players in the orchestra with the conductor too – and even the tips of the instruments exactly as would be seen by the audience.

The drawing of the man in the theatre box (overleaf) may have been another outcome of the same evening's outing to the opera. It is an example of Gerard's instinct for composition. He knew exactly where to place the box on the page and skilfully uses the caption and his signature in order to indicate its position aloft.

The family were still taking holidays, and one year Gerard managed to add to the general excitement by contracting appendicitis on the island of Sylt in the North Sea. Prompt action ensured his survival and recovery. His mother mentions that he insisted for a long time on wearing his appendix round his neck like an amulet. This piece of his anatomy must also have survived the journey to England for Gerard told me in a letter that it was confiscated at Highgate School one day when he produced it at lunch.

On Sylt he found the brass bands on the promenade irresistible and it was from Gerard that I first heard of the practice of small boys who torment brass players by standing nearby sucking lemons, thereby increasing their saliva output to such an extent that further playing becomes impossible. I have no doubt that he spoke from experience.

Shortly before we were married, Gerard met up with his father on Sylt and sent me this postcard.

Hilde and Ludwig must have been considering the possibility of leaving Germany, for in another letter to her sister at the time of the Nazi invasion of Austria she relates her thankfulness that the family did not decide to make Vienna their new home. In the event they finally left Berlin as late as December 1938, their destination being Florence. This uprooting from a deeply ingrained cultural environment and from the security and physical comforts of an established home was a burden for his parents, but fortunately for Gerard the move into exile does not seem to have been the traumatic experience it might have been. His headmistress, Vera Lachmann, wrote him the following sad letter which indicates that, in the end, their departure had been a fairly sudden decision.

Meine liebe gute Landplage,
Mein Loki!

Die Loge

Drawn at the age of eleven years.

Yesterday I received a letter from your mother – please thank her very much for it. It says that you will not return to school. It is sad that we could not properly see each other before you left, but, maybe, it is better like that because it would not have been easy for either of us.

You know, Loki, that I have worried about you and was unhappy about many things: your inattentiveness and lack of discipline, your inability quietly to submit and fall in with others, your lazy unreliability, your secret love for anything that is deformed, tortuous and unnatural. But all the same I shall miss you, because I know that you are goodhearted and suffer with all those who suffer and that sometimes you hear the soft and secret beat of the all-pervading pulse of the world. I hope that your great gifts will bring joy to yourself and other people. I have often thought that deep down, Loki, we understand each other as if I were your older sister. I also know your fears: you never fear that anything could happen to you, but only that there is something frightening that exists. I also think I understand the fun you have in oscillating through the legs of all these dignified good men, who so seriously look over their paunches, and in poking fun at their dignified ideals. I don't want you to become a waster, but to become an artist – that means: work, work, work, work. I don't want you to become a conductor or a designer but an actor. I tell you this today although it is too early, because I do not know whether we shall meet again. The diversity of your many gifts is a danger. You must decide on one route, otherwise you will fail. We will always miss you, Helmut most of all.

Deine Vera Lachmann. –

Gerard's mother writes in lighter vein:
*For Gerard Berlin is finished because his friend
Heinz has gone to live in Florence.*

She must have been extremely thankful for such a happy outcome
of events. Heinz, the son of a teacher at the Lachmann School, she
describes as a charming rascal. He spoke fluent Italian and knew all
the museums in the city; Gerard's one desire was to join him and to
be introduced to both.

En route for Florence and despite what must have been a time of
upheaval, the family still managed to spend a relaxed time in St
Moritz where, in three sentences, Hilde sets the scene:
*It is heavenly here, quite unimaginably beautiful – there's no place like
it. Gerard decorates the ice rink with his drawings which leave everybody quite speechless. He speaks Switzer-Deutsch, is friends with everybody from the head waiter to the cleaner (whom he supplies with rolls
and fruit he has pinched from the table), knows everyone around because
he either talks to them or they to him, and looks like a posaunen engel.*

This comparison of Gerard with a trombone angel caught my eye,
for one of my favourite among his childhood drawings has that title
and I think the young Gerd must have been aware of his mother's
term of endearment.

My future parents-in-law clearly intended to make Italy their

Drawn at the age of
twelve years.

home. The family rented a flat in Pensione Gaselli on the Lugano while looking around for more permanent accommodation. They chose a villa in the country between Florence and Fiesole, with a garden and a view over the city, where in due course their German furniture arrived and was installed. For a short time it may have seemed that life was settling down, though it cannot have taken long for them to be aware of the fast-changing political situation, and the troubles looming, which once again would affect their lives.

Gerard soon had to leave the German school he was attending in Florence after Hitler's decree that German schools were no longer allowed to accept Jewish pupils. At this time Hilde describes her son thus:

He is now at the unruly adolescent stage. He is cheeky and as usual his work is not up to standard because of all the changes of schools, school books and the long gaps in between. Surprisingly he has adapted his behaviour to this new strictly disciplined school, but at home he is all the more unruly. He is good-looking, tall, strong, on the fat side and curses a lot in Italian. He only obeys after he has exhausted us. He has a new teacher, the first violinist of an orchestra here who teaches him conducting, a lot of theory he did not know, and many more interesting things. Gerard feels quite pleased with himself and thinks we are hard on him. It is not altogether easy with this creature. His imagination is still flourishing and looks for new stimuli of which Florence can provide plenty. Even I am not quite free from its spell.

An unpleasant episode occurred when Ludwig was away briefly in Palestine. Rumours abounded of a forthcoming plan of Hitler's to visit Mussolini in Rome and of a decision to intern all Jews living in Italy for the period of time that the Führer was in the country.

Gerard's mother acted promptly and left with him immediately for the mountains. 'Good thing we left,' she wrote in a letter, 'because they came to look for us.'

She added:

I had to prepare Gerard for the possibility of internment and as you can understand, everything I have achieved is undone. Once more he is frightened, asks for his bedroom door to be kept open at night and the light left on. He is distracted and lacks concentration. I am upset about him.

These events sparked off discussion as his parents debated the best course to take for the future. The idea of emigrating to Palestine appealed to Gerard's father, his own father having recently left

Berlin to settle in Haifa. Hilde was reluctant to consider that prospect but was persuaded, nevertheless, to look at the country and journeyed there to see for herself. Although agreeably surprised by many things she found there, she clearly decided that the educational facilities it offered were not at all what she wanted for her son.

In all probability the decision that the family should split up was made with the intention of it being a temporary measure. Hilde and Gerard were to go to England and Ludwig to Palestine; he would rejoin them when the future had become a little clearer and circumstances more predictable. It seemed a reasonable enough decision. Ludwig's father had opened a small bank in Haifa and was understandably eager to have his son around at the start of the venture. Hilde's sister and brother-in-law were already in England, also some friends. She would not be alone. Above all, the schools were highly recommended. They were not to know that the war and the immobility it enforced were to make the parting more or less permanent.

In London the Hoffnungs, mother and son, set up home, renting 5 Thornton Way in Hampstead Garden Suburb on the northern outskirts of central London. It was to be his home for the rest of his life. In time their heavy, finely-made, much-travelled German furniture arrived. It demanded far larger rooms than the reasonably-sized ones in which it now found itself, and appeared ponderous and a little awkward.

Gerard's mother chose this house for two reasons. She liked the line of poplar trees at the bottom of the garden, and it also had central heating, not so common at that time as it is today. She was to be doubly disappointed, for within the year the council removed the poplar trees which were disturbing the foundations of nearby flats and, alas, the central heating never functioned properly. In war-time England there was little that could be done to improve the situation.

For a short time Gerard attended Bunce Court, a school which had recently been set up to care for German refugee children in Kent where his uncle, Hilde's brother-in-law, taught art. At this school, in the depths of the country, Gerard was surrounded by children in a similar situation or much worse, many having been dispatched alone to England by parents desperate to get them to safety at all costs. Here he was provided with a breathing space in which to become more gradually acclimatised to life in a new country.

The school was run by a German lady, Anna Essinger, helped by two of her sisters and other staff. For many of the refugee children it was the only home they had at that time. Gerard was his usual ebullient self, and Anna Essinger managed to tolerate him for two terms before pronouncing that he must leave. That there was no disgrace attached to this decision is clear from the warm welcome he received on a number of return visits he made to the school. Many years later, shortly after we were married, we lunched with Anna Essinger and her sisters who were then living in Finchley in North London, and their affection for Gerard had not waned – nor their memories of his misdemeanours which they related to me with glee. At the time his antics were greatly enjoyed by the pupils but, understandably, were not appreciated by the staff. One night, a teacher retiring to her room was horrified to find a child in blood-stained night attire lying outside her door. As, faint with horror, she knelt to investigate what heinous crime had been committed, the figure stood up, nodded and walked away. It was, of course, Gerard, who had soaked the child's pyjamas in a bottleful of red ink especially purchased for the purpose.

His habit of continually playing his saxophone about the school drove the headmistress to distraction. Eventually she explained to him that not all people enjoyed the sounds he produced, and he was forbidden to play the instrument in the school building. That after-noon groups of children, attracted by the familiar sound, were seen staring at a dormitory window high up in the school building where a small figure could be seen. Again it was Gerard, perched precari-ously on the window sill, legs dangling outside, obeying the letter if not the spirit of the law.

The story that Gerard in turn told of Anna Essinger was of the day on which she inadvertently opened the door of a lavatory he was occupying at the time. Undeterred she took one look at him and said, 'Sit up!'

In September 1939, in his fourteenth year, he became a pupil at Highgate School. War had broken out and the greater part of this London school had been evacuated to the West Country.

Mr Twidell, Headmaster of Highgate School in London, retains unblurred memories of Gerard at that time.
Hoffnung was ruddy faced, good-looking, very well mannered and smiling. He settled down quickly. He seemed generally to be wearing Boy Scouts' uniform, because he was a messenger at a First Aid Post in Golders Green. He was one of about eight boys in the first term and he attracted some attention by his curious voice, his drawings and his gaiety. He bothered monitors by petty infringements of rules, but there was no particular clash with authority. . . . After two terms 'Highgate School at Highgate' reached one hundred and twenty boys. In a building which could hold six

Drawn in 1957 and published in the Highgate School magazine together with an interview for a series on famous old boys.

hundred, they rattled like peas: here staffing problems began to grow: here Mrs Hoffnung paid the first of various visits, worrying somewhat about the academic progress and reports of Gerard. It was not easy to reassure her in these respects, nor was it of comfort to her to know, what she knew well, that Gerard had remarkable talent in drawing. She was the nicest and kindest of women, eager for her son's progress. Unfortunately, even if she might be feeling severe about Gerard, he was generally able to make her laugh.

Mrs Hoffnung worried so much about Gerard's progress that she arranged for one of the senior boys to coach him. These periods were hardly a success, because after a few minutes Gerard's thoughts turned to music and he would insist upon playing the piano. His coach was conscientious enough shortly to tell Mrs Hoffnung that her son would not and could not be coached.

Mr Twidell goes on:

A caricature of a master at Highgate School.

Hoffnung played games as little as he could. He boasted that the only time he kicked a football it burst. He listened with great seriousness to criticism and admonition, and he liked to show that he had responded, particularly if there was originality in his response. The length of his hair had received comment in various quarters. He arrived one day with a Prussian haircut. There is a memory of his riding to school one day on an incredible German bicycle, with huge red tyres like German sausages, which might have come out of one of his cartoons.

Towards the end of his first year he began to disturb the balance of certain masters. Most of the young masters had left for Service and their replacements were less capable of dealing with humorists and jesters. A situation was reached when 'all masters taking Hoffnung' were asked to send him immediately to the Master-in-Charge if he upset the discipline of their Forms. Hoffnung also was warned. He reached the Master-in-Charge fairly soon, who, having little time to listen to Hoffnung in cajoling mood, told him to bend over. On the second occasion when he was sent from the room, he entered the quarters of the Master-in-Charge and looked up at him with head down and rueful expression. 'Get it over quick please sir,' he said. Having had his beating, he shook hands and left rubbing his backside, a beam of happiness on his face and all guilt removed.

One day he visited the Master-in-Charge, looking worried and unhappy.

'What do you want, Hoffnung?'

'I want you to beat me, sir.'

'Why?'

'Oh sir, I'm in very bed [he could not manage the short "a" at this stage] trouble and I know that it will come to you.

Please, sir, will you beat me? I want to get it over.'

The Master-in-Charge then said, 'No, Hoffnung, I will not beat you, whatever you have done, and I shall never beat you again.'

Hoffnung went away sadly, wondering how in the future, guilt could be expiated. It is probable that this incident took place after an exploit which he often recalled. He brought a violin to school, and having discovered a trap door under the floor of the Science Lecture Room, he secreted himself there and played snatches while one of the temporary masters was teaching a Form. He said afterwards that his worst moment was when the Master-in-Charge, who had been summoned, stopped and looking down at a hole in the floorboards, failed to see the anxious eye looking up through the hole.

Hoffnung knew instinctively which boys were good to and for their fellows, and which were not. He knew which boys required help and encouragement and which boys could stand up to normal school life.

(This observation tallies well with a remark made earlier by the headmistress of Gerard's school in Berlin who wrote, 'He was infinitely good-natured, made friends with the most unpopular fellow-pupils and bravely took their part, generously gave them half his lunch and let them play with his toys and musical instruments.')

Mr Twidell concludes his reminiscences:

Hoffnung was not academic, and there was no attempt, on the last of Mrs Hoffnung's visits, to persuade her against her somewhat reluctant decision to let him go to an Art School. When he left, there was a great gap. Disturbers of the peace and eccentrics and possessors of gusto may not be treated with the awe and respect that attends athletes and, occasionally, scholars, but they are remembered and discussed by their contemporaries long afterwards and remain a legend. It was sad that Hoffnung was known as a boy to so few masters and boys of Highgate School, but it is possible that his schooldays were more appreciated by him under their abnormal circumstances than they would have been if he had been one among six hundred.

Gerard devoted much of his spare time, as a Scout messenger, attached to a suburb air-raid post. Here he is seen wearing his badge.

HIGHGATE SCHOOL.

..........Third......Term 19 4 1

Name.............Hoffnung G.....................

Final Place......2 0.......in..............B.:.......Form.

SUBJECTS OF STUDY.	RANK IN FORM.	NUMBER OF BOYS IN FORM.	AVERAGE AGE OF BOYS.	REPORT.
Latin				
~~Greek or German~~ Biology	9	13	15.1	Very poor. Will make no progress until he pays more attention to his work, and puts much more energy into it.
~~Divinity~~ Chemistry	24	25	14.5	Very weak. Very inattentive. Must work much harder.
English History	20	25	14.5	Very weak, but somewhat improved.
English Literature	21	25	14.5	His Examination was very poor, but his term work was better.
Geography	23	25	14.5	Fair. Works well.
Natural Science Physics	18	25	14.5	Made a greater effort of late. Must develop a more serious interest in the subject
French	15	25	14.5	Fair.
Mathematics DIVISION Set III	21	23	14.5	Fair. Now making good progress, but very restless.
Drawing	Music—Vocal		Instrumental	

Form Master's General Report He has improved considerably, but lacks seriousness of purpose for any space of time. Life is not a continuous Cartoon!

House Tutor's Report He is more serious than he was, but is not yet serious enough. Improving.

..................................Head Master.

..................................Form Master.

..................................House Tutor.

N.B.   G—Good.   F—Fair.   M—Moderate.   B—Bad.   V—Very.

Holiday Work......Certificate Revision..

Next Term begins........................, ends........................

Boarders return........................, not later than 8 p.m.

Every Boy must appear punctually on the appointed day, except in case of illness, or some urgent reason to be notified beforehand by letter to the Head Master.

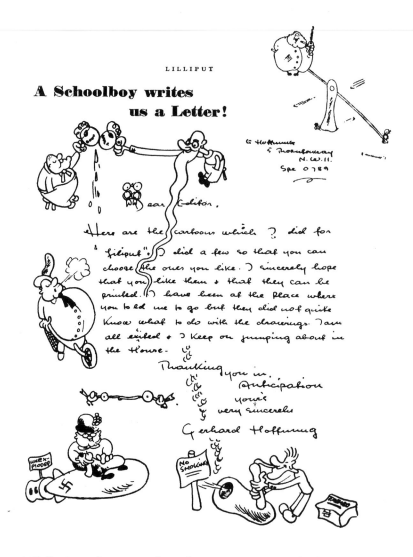

While Gerard may not have been serious enough about his academic progress he was, however, resolute about his drawing. The previous year, at the age of fifteen, he had written a letter to the editor of *Lilliput*, that pocket-sized magazine of excellent quality. The letter was reproduced in facsimile together with some of his cartoons and was his very first publication. This was enormously encouraging and marked in some fundamental way a change in his approach to drawing. Now it was no longer a hobby but an activity to be shared with many: no longer an indulgence but a professional pursuit.

Encouragement was not always forthcoming and sometimes Gerard did not get the reassurance he needed. At much the same time he visited Walter Trier, the doyen of German cartoonists and illustrators, also a German-Jewish refugee in London. I can only imagine

... and here are the Schoolboy's Cartoons

"*And this is my husband*"

"Oh! Speak Again, Bright Angel"

"*I'm Nobody's Baby*"

Hyde Park Orator

The Boy Who Knew the Answer

that the reason Trier was unhelpful and uncomplimentary, advising Gerard that he believed there to be no future for him as an artist, was because at that particular time Gerard's style was very influenced by Trier, as can be seen in the drawings done while at Highgate School. Perhaps he took offence at this. David Low's criticism, on the other hand, was constructive and caring, as can be seen from his letter to Mr Roberts who was the manager of *The New Statesman* at the time. (Mr Roberts had passed Gerard's drawings on to David Low as a favour.)

Herewith I return the drawings of your young friend. I think he has talent which he might develop successfully. It seems to me (but it might be only my prejudice) that he over-exaggerates his caricature, and takes too much youthful delight in the elementary 'humour' of gross misshapen forms. To me his work would be more pleasing were he to discipline and

balance emphasis; to learn to draw more solidly – to give more body to the work – to be less super- ficial; and to draw compositions of figures assem- bled in a setting of some kind. One gets awfully tired of single figures standing in nothing. All these comments indicate just my personal taste – no more. In art every man should be a rule to himself and no man should take advice from another.

By early 1943 Gerard's sojourn at Art School, or Schools to be precise, had started. It was not an inspiring time for him. Predictably he was not interested in the normal curriculum provided for stu- dents and found routine tedious. Ann Gould, a friend and fellow student at Hornsey College of Art, describes the atmosphere and events, together with their outcome:

(Absent-minded young man whose umbrella dropped on the train to a lady): 'Could you kindly hold on for me for a second?'

I remember Gerard coming to Art School, I think in 1942. All the London schools had been evacuated. But as Hornsey is in Middlesex, it was left to carry on, with the added interests of fire-watching rota and air-raid warnings.

The Monday morning that Gerard Hoffnung was brought into the Antique Class by an unsuspecting teacher, was the beginning of a livelier phase of study for most of us. To begin with, he lacked the unease that usually lay on new students. He was unintimidated by the staff – and by the students. He was unimpressed by the silent monotonal room, coated with layers of heavy white plaster dust, where the giant sightless figures towered over us on their grey boxes and were manoeuvred about on squeaky castors.

If it had not occurred to us that we could, after all, draw the casts as we didn't see them, Hoffnung soon suggested it by covering his paper with a series of small grotesque figures, with umbrellas, geysers and civil defence insignia, while we were still striving to fit enormous seven- foot statues onto large sheets of cartridge paper.

Only four or five of us became close friends of his: the boys were par- ticularly suspicious of his humour, his indifference to authority, and his determination. Though he was the same age as we were, he differed from us all in already knowing just what he wanted to learn.

He resented being forced to spend days on general subjects that pre- vented him from specialising. His direction was set, and he wanted to get on with the job. If some of the staff insisted on treating him like a schoolboy, and dismissed the possibilities of his interest in caricature, they had only themselves to blame if he, in turn, retaliated like an irre- pressible fourth-former.

The school was run rather like a country house, where we were all expected to be on our best behaviour. Hoffnung broke all the rules, and questioned them publicly, irreverently and insistently. The animosity he roused in others was sometimes very apparent. His behaviour was not always a counter-attack, but a challenge. I think he may have been afraid of shyness, in himself and others, and his way of overcoming it was to make the initial move. It established his mood as the prevailing tone, and once there, it was other people's reactions that were under observation, not his own – a clever defence, in chess or in life.

At school, he enjoyed most of what went on. We had expeditions to the zoo, where the animals began to acquire the expressions of some of the staff, once he had caricatured them. But Hoffnung's satire was never directed against his friends, he was extremely kind and spontaneous. We enjoyed his company tremendously. There was a nice legend, that must remain apocryphal, as I don't know anyone who actually saw this: Hoffnung had drawn a wickedly hyperbolic drawing of our Top Model, seen from the rear. It was pinned up in the Life Room where he produced a pea-shooter, and proceeded to bombard it on all flanks, with great accuracy. It worried the students, even as a story. A dangerous sort of leg-pull. Even risqué. It left them uncomfortable at the sacriligiousness of the idea, at the vengeance it would surely provoke from some quarter.

There had been constant threats and rows with the Head, who found Gerard's attitude to authority unforgivable, and, less understandably, disapproved of his dedication to the art of caricature. Humour was certainly not a thing they had in common. I suspect that the Head felt it was a degradation of art, an inclination which should be discouraged and stamped out. We had seen him enraged by Gerard, but I still didn't

Drawn at the age of sixteen years.

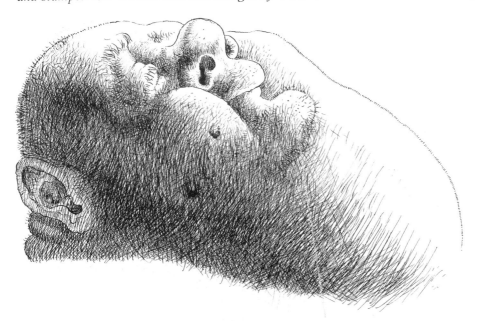

believe it when Gerard announced that he had been expelled.
He was bubbling over with glee, and gave an enthralling and realistic
account of the interview, in mime and sound.

From my memory of Gerard's recollections, he was also outraged and unhappy at this outcome, a reaction he probably kept to himself at the time. The attitude of the Head of Hornsey School of Art towards Gerard was in direct contrast to the understanding and fellow-feeling he had experienced when he was at school. Former students I have spoken to remember Mr Moody as a somewhat humourless man, lacking in imagination. Several suspected him of anti-Semitism. Given such traits, it is no wonder he found Gerard difficult to tolerate.

Jean Atkinson, another fellow-student at Hornsey, felt that:
Hornsey in those days certainly wasn't ready for a Gerard Hoffnung.
I'm sure nobody on the staff knew how to take him. Russell Reeve was
the only teacher who was friendly to him.

Jean was one of the students who enjoyed Gerard's antics:
His friendship meant a great deal to me as he was such a super person.
It was his eccentricity and humour which I enjoyed most. . . . On one
occasion I was being taken by my
parents to the Waldorf Hotel to
dinner to meet some old friends of
theirs. Such grand hotels were a bit
out of my scope in those days and
when we were sitting in the large
lounge talking to my parents'
friends, a page boy came through
calling my name. I couldn't believe
my ears at first, then was highly
embarrassed. Anyway, I was wanted
on the telephone and by guess who?

After his expulsion from Hornsey, another mishap awaited him. As an enemy alien Gerard was not allowed to join the Forces and was therefore directed into a reserved occupation. He was awaiting notification of a teaching post when, due to some muddle with his papers, he was summarily ordered to work as a bottle-washer at the Express Dairy farm at Finchley, not far from his home. He could only have been there for a short time, but the experience remained vividly etched on his memory and, incidentally, provided some hilarious stories for his repertoire. Very early morning starts, bitterly cold war-time conditions and the companionship of elderly men, too old for military service, who teased and ragged him mercilessly, were far from ideal. The description of the catastrophic results when he inadvertently reversed the bottle-washing machine, and of his efforts at milking cows never failed to convulse an audience. He had a small scar on his forehead which he assured me was the result of a wound suffered on the very first occasion he tried to milk a cow. Unsuccessful at expressing any milk, he overestimated the elasticity of the udder and, when it suddenly sprang from his grasp and bounced back to its normal position, the poor cow, much aggrieved, promptly kicked him.

In due course, Gerard was relieved of his dairy duties, and was allowed to take up a teaching post. In April 1945, just twenty years old, he found himself en route for Stamford School in Lincolnshire whose noted pupils in the past had included Sir Malcolm Sargent and Sir Michael Tippett. Some time ago when I gave a lecture at the school I met the art teacher whose pregnancy at the time had created the temporary vacancy filled by Gerard.

Although he did not enjoy teaching, his eccentricities made him very popular with the boys. They looked forward to his classes, not least to being entertained from his fund of hyperbolic nonsense stories. Little wonder that he was heckled unmercifully and found discipline difficult to maintain. One way in which he enticed the boys to good behaviour was to threaten *not* to play his bassoon to them at the end of the lesson, a warning, it seems, that never failed to achieve its desired effect. This instrument was appropriated for the duration of his stay from the wife of one of the masters, and he could be heard practising in the Art Room in the evenings. The hours he spent improvising at the organ of All Saints Church in the town were more satisfying and dramatic. Others remember that he sometimes played a violin, which suggests that his early lessons on this instrument cannot have been entirely without effect.

Much of his time was spent drawing. In his small office attached to the Art Room he worked during the evenings and would spend hours, first pencilling in the elaborate details and then inking them in with a fine mapping pen. A former pupil, Philip Towell, remembers an occasion when Gerard had left a pencilled drawing lying on his table and returned to find that some thoughtless prankster had totally erased his hours of hard work. His reaction was more one of puzzlement than anger. 'What a silly thing to do. Why do you think anyone should do that?' He took no steps to find the culprit.

Some months later he wrote to his friend, Jean Atkinson:
I am now on the editorial staff of the Stamford Mercury *which claims to be the oldest newspaper in Britain, so I am really doing three or four full jobs at once with teaching, newspaper work,* Lilliput, *book illustrations etc. The* Evening News *in London want me to join their staff permanently, that's why I may have to leave Stamford and live in London.*

In any event, he packed his bags at the end of his second term and returned to live at home in Thornton Way. Here he continued his work, establishing himself as a free-lance cartoonist. For some time he had been developing a style that was no longer linear using stark black and white to create an illusion of depth, and in doing so had achieved some sort of third dimension. In 1946 he did a drawing of

an old man with gout, one of his blackest. It illustrates the detail and
the immense amount of pen-scratching that went into his work at the
time. Also, his lakeside scene, bursting with activity, is a feast for
the eye and bears endless scrutiny.

It must have been about this time, when they were all in their
early twenties, that Gerald Priestland remembers Gerard coming to
Oxford to visit him and his wife-to-be Sylvia who had been at
Hornsey Art College with Gerard. Gerry recalls:
*I cannot remember much about the visit except that half-way across the
Great Quadrangle of Christ Church he stopped a venerable academic and*

enquired whether he were a professor. He was, it transpired, of Pastoral
Theology, or Christian Apologetics, or Hermeneutics or some such.
'Splendid,' said Gerard, shaking him warmly by the hand. 'Well done.
Keep it up!' And we left the professor looking more encouraged than he
had felt for years.

By the age of twenty-two, at about the time this photograph was
taken at his drawing board, his work was in wide circulation and
was appearing in publications such as *Lilliput*, *Housewife*, *The*
Strand, *Tatler* and other magazines.

His drawings, carefree, kindly and gentle, brimming with life and
humour, were received with special delight in the post-war restrictions and constraints of power-cuts and rationing.

In a radio talk he once spoke about the structure of these cartoons:
My little chaps may be ugly and sometimes quite vicious-looking, but on
the whole they are amiable fellows with Christmas puddings inside them
– at least that is what I like to think they are. They put up with one
another and with me with exemplary resignation. None of them ever bit
me or lunged at me with an open sardine tin, and I would never allow
that sort of behaviour to go on. . . . Even when I draw a really horrible
old monster I greet his arrival with affection and tolerance, and I give
him a cup of tea or a basinful of blood or a saucer of cement to drink
before he sits down. Ah, indeed, there is one sitting outside right at this
moment waiting to be drawn, and if he's polite – and I sincerely hope he
will be – he will take off his hat and say 'Merry Christmas'.

He spent a brief period teaching Art at Harrow School where
Nicolas Bentley made his acquaintance. Nicolas had been asked to
judge a handwriting competition when the master accompanying
him was called away for some reason or other.

I went on looking at the entries by myself – or so I thought – until I realized that there was someone else in the room, someone I could hear but could not see because there were screens between us.

As I moved around from one set of entries to another, this audible but invisible presence seemed to follow me, and after a while, simply out of curiosity, I sneaked back on my tracks and moved abruptly round the corner of a screen.

That was my first sight of Gerard — at a distance of about four inches.

Gerard always struck me as being in most respects a little larger than life, and this impression seemed to be magnified by my coming upon him so suddenly at such close quarters. He goggled for a moment — I dare say I did too — then introduced himself, in those high scholastic tones that were part of the act of being Hoffnung. It was an act that I never got tired of seeing or hearing and it amused me as much on our first impact — or what would have been an impact if he hadn't been standing still when I rounded the screen — as it did the last time I saw him.

It's an easy and consequently a popular compliment to pay an artist to say that his work is original, as though there were some mysterious merit in originality itself. But if you divorce it from purpose, originality hasn't much value and usually less interest.

But Gerard was a true original, both as a man and an artist. I think he knew quite well when certain of his eccentricities were comic, but there were others of which I think he was less well aware. The mannerisms that endeared him to millions on TV and radio, of a man much older than in fact he was, were not all assumed. The air of abstraction, the glinting glance that reminded one of a Teutonic Pickwick, the high and sudden laughter were the reflection of a genuine and quite unusual personality.

I do not know why Gerard's appearance should have been at such variance with his age, though sometimes I think it may have had to do with the fact that by the time he was twenty, his hair was already receding; and that in a very short time much of it had disappeared altogether. He seemed unconcerned and not at all upset by this, but perhaps involuntarily he used it as a prop to age his persona.

I certainly remember on three different occasions being taken for Gerard's daughter. The first time this happened, it took me some time to make out why it was that a young man with whom I was in conversation, should declare that he had been at school with my father!

In the spring of 1948, when Gerard was teaching at Harrow School, his mother died. While the result of her prolonged illness was predictable, her death was a dreadful shock to him. They had been devoted to

each other; she had been his mentor, his critic, his inspiration and the one person who understood his talents and aspirations and had carefully nursed his development – empirically in his childhood and with judicious indulgence during his adolescence and early maturity. They understood, respected and adored each other, and provided unquestioning mutual support.

Illness had forestalled any possibility of Hilde joining her husband, now a successful banker in Israel, and six months before her death Ludwig Hoffnung came to London in order to be with her. Afterwards he returned to Israel.

Gerard's relationship with his father was not an easy one. I think my father-in-law was proud of his son's success without perhaps understanding its substance. Certainly they were closer at a distance than in proximity, and the affection that I know Gerard felt for his father seemed often to be undermined by exasperation and aggravation when they were together. I had the opportunity to observe this close at hand, though only fleetingly, for my meetings with Gerard's father were few; once very briefly during my early acquaintance with Gerard, and on two other occasions when we met during holidays on the continent – not more than a few days in all. I think the reason for their discord was most likely an unbreachable gulf of understanding between their two totally different characters and

An illustration to the story of Susanna and the Elders.

This is positively the last
time that I shall ever
fly in an aeroplane. A
svelling experience. I
shudder to think of tomorrow.
Athens – Lydda (if I ever get
there). Rome: the most
wonderful experience in my
life. Would'nt mind spending
three weeks here & then
back to old London by
boat. Hope you are
all well, Cocks. Women
in Rome nearly as beauti-
ful as Mrs. A. My regards
to old Wiggins (Louise).
          Signore Hoffnung.

Signore Bruno Adler
Signora Bella Ilse Adler,
10 Oakhillpark,
Hampstead
London, N.W.3.
England, –

ITALIA 25 LIRE
POSTA AEREA

E. Richter - Roma

worlds. The practical formality of one and the extrovert gregarious-
ness of the other made it difficult for them to get on. Ludwig Hoffnung died in 1955, a short time after the birth of our son whom,
sadly, he never saw.

Gerard visited his father in Israel in 1948. On his journey he flew
for the first and only time. It was an experience which he found
nerve-wracking and one he determined never to repeat. I think he
was genuinely unhappy during the time he was airborne, but typi-
cally, the whole saga of this flight to Israel was relished over the
years, and when related to an audience was hilarious. On that occasion, stopping in Rome for two or three days, he met up with his
friend, the painter Lawrence Scarfe. He also sent a card to Ilse and
Bruno Adler.

The illustrations to the story of Susanna and the Elders show us
Gerard's first rumbustuous contributions to the world of legends.
Then with equally uninhibited zest he produced his own particular
version of the *Odyssey*, where Nausicaa is given the role of a rowdy
tomboy battling against her graceless handmaidens on the rugger
field. Odysseus, lashed to the mast with his ears well plugged, is
confronted by a raucous mob of amiable troll-like creatures alias the
sirens, and Penelope's suitors swipe at each other with umbrellas and
frying pans.

Gerard, by now just twenty-three years old, was far removed from
the child who only ten years previously had been a pupil at school
in Germany. During the intervening years he had lived for some
months in one country, settled in another, learned to speak a new
language without a trace of an accent, received in some measure a
public school and college education and, more importantly, had

Hoffnung

established himself as a free-lance cartoonist. In just over another ten years he was to complete his lifespan.

Now in London, immersed in his work and on his own, Gerard set about engaging a housekeeper. He always maintained that Marie 'just turned up on my doorstep one day carrying a suitcase and a large feather eiderdown'. It is possible to believe this, for had he searched the world over he could not have found anyone who fitted the post so well. Then in her late fifties, Marie had come to England from Germany shortly before the war with a Jewish family, though she herself was not Jewish. She was a round, rosy-cheeked little woman with grey hair pulled up into a bun at the top of her head. She had a sense of humour and at times a wicked temper, and her little face would screw up in delight or fury, depending on whether Gerard was entertaining her or driving her to distraction. She hated Hitler with venom, dreamed of old Berlin and the Kaiser Wilhelm, spoke very little English and adored Gerard's cat. The house was run simply and meticulously by Marie, who produced meals that belied the rationing restrictions of the time and ironed Gerard's shirts with an expertise that spoilt him for ever after.

Odysseus watches Nausicaa playing ba with her handmaidens.

Gerard and Marie had a lively, sometimes fiery relationship. 'Mr 'Offnung, he a vair naudie boy' she would say to me, her little face puckered up with rage; and certainly this was often the case. She inspired him to play pranks. It was her habit to go down to the kitchen around nine o'clock in the evening, returning upstairs with a steaming jug of coffee. The short absence from her room generally proved to be an irresistible temptation to Gerard. Sometimes it was the simple idea of a cushion balanced on top of her door to fall upon her as she entered the room. Once I remember he actually secreted himself beneath her large feather eiderdown so that, having reached, as she thought, the haven of her room, shut and locked the door against intrusion and put down her jug of coffee, she received the shock of her life as an eerie muffled laugh issued from her bed.

Marie stayed with us for two years after our marriage. She coped well with the change my presence inevitably made, but life was not the same for her. She became an old-age pensioner and worked only part-time for us. Although we had a genuine affection for her I think we were sometimes, quite unintentionally, thoughtless, and she in her turn could be exceedingly difficult. She was broken-hearted at the death of Gerard's cat. There were dark moments and one day, in a temper, she left us. I was pregnant and I think the idea of yet another intrusion into the household was too much for her. We found out where she was living, but she wouldn't come to see us until one day Gerard passed her in the car, dramatically waylaid her and

drove with her to Thornton Way. She met our baby son and was delighted to do so. She visited us again a short while after that, and we could scarcely believe it when we heard soon afterwards that she had died suddenly in her bed.

As he sat at his drawing board, increasingly involved and complicated fantasies tumbled from Gerard's pen onto the paper. In 1949 came perhaps the most intricate of all, a drawing for the poster advertising a popular film of the day, *Passport to Pimlico*. I do

Gerard's housekeeper, Marie.

A poster advertising a popular film of the day, *Passport to Pimlico*, 1949.

Lilliput.

not have the original design but it is unlikely to have been larger than 12″ × 15″, and to squeeze so much into so little space is no mean achievement. He drew a pretty surround for the title page of *Lilliput*, and for *Housewife* magazine, a poor little centipede wife darning hundreds of her husband's socks as he sits comfortably in front of the fire reading a copy of the *Centipede's Gazette*. Later, he produced two other drawings on a centipede theme. This too was the year that saw his first exhibition, at the Little Gallery in Piccadilly.

He also visited Ireland, and Quidnunc of *The Irish Times* had this to say:

At present, Mr Hoffnung is in Dublin, looking for a leprechaun.

You would expect, from his drawings, to find in Mr Hoffnung a frail, twisted old man, with a pronounced stoop and straggling white hair. Instead, you meet a well-built, almost athletic young man of 24 years of age, who wears a trench coat, and carries a walking stick, which he continually brandishes to underline points in the conversation.

That is the first surprise. The second comes later, when he speaks. Instead of the robust, hearty chat one might have expected from his appearance, he talks like something straight out of one of his own drawings, in a vague, absent-minded manner, frequently losing the thread of the discourse.

Mr Hoffnung is a wonderful man to interview, helpful and co-operative all the way. 'You can describe my appearance for a start,' he said, pointing out that most people, like myself, expect a much older man. 'You can say that I'm pinkish. It's true, you know, in a way.'

Then, his hobbies. Mr Hoffnung has exactly the sort of hobbies that look well in a newspaper interview, and he has them all at his fingertips. Pipe-smoking is one of them. He not only smokes a pipe in a positive, serious manner – the way other people collect stamps, or go fishing – but he also collects pipes. And he collects cats, although at the moment his stock is low. Turkish baths he also lists among his favourite spare-time occupations.

It was on the subject of Turkish baths that I first came up against his vague, absent-minded habit of dropping a subject. He had started to tell me an incident concerning his first Turkish bath – 'it took place during the "blitz"' – when suddenly he broke off. 'No,' he said. 'I'm sorry. It would really take far too long to tell you that story. I'll just finish it there.'

Yet another of his hobbies is playing the bassoon. For a time, he played not only the bassoon, but also the violin and percussion instruments in an amateur orchestra; but lately he has been too busy to do any more than an occasional bassoon solo. 'For the cats,' he added. 'Will that do, or do you want any more spare-time interests?' he asked. 'For instance, I play practical jokes on my friends. I always have. I used to get into trouble over it at school, where I was beaten regularly, every

Two from a series of drawings of Turkish baths.

Saturday, on the general principle that I had probably done something during the week to justify it. Indeed, they were quite right. I usually had.'

In contrast to the rest of his work at this time he painted a small water-colour – a little knot of trees on Hampstead Heath, one of his very few serious paintings or drawings. Gerard gave this as a present to his friend, Henri Henrion, who at that time was art editor of a publication called *Contact Books*. Henri had recently engaged Gerard as his assistant and recalls that it took only two weeks for them both to realise that it was not the happiest relationship for either of them. Needless to say, Gerard's help complicated tasks that were easy to begin with. Another drawing linked with the Heath was made jointly by Gerard and the *Punch* artist, Rowland Emett. Gerard was a great admirer of Emett's work. He and Rowland had met and become close friends and together they drew a picture after one of their outings together. Oddly, there is no mention of this meeting in Gerard's diary though there is mention of a dinner together two days previously. Gerard's diaries date back to 1946. They are mostly of similar design, leather, very small, measuring barely $2\frac{1}{4}''$ by $3\frac{1}{4}''$. Those differing from the normal pattern are even smaller. They were usually produced from his waistcoat pocket. Inside, the entries are brief and the writing, of necessity, miniscule. They have been useful in checking dates and have revived my memory of a few forgotten events. They contain names that over the years have faded into the past. Others such as Donald Swann, Gerald Priestland, John Amis and the Emetts, are, after nearly forty years, still at hand as good friends. It is the three or four diaries that he kept before I knew him that I find most nostalgic, perhaps because he was so young at the time. They also help to paint a picture of his life then. An entry on 22 March 1947 (incidentally his birthday) notes that he attended a rehearsal of I T M A, Tommy Handley's superbly funny radio programme, which Gerard illustrated in the *Radio Times*. On 5

Drawings announcing Tommy Handley's programme in *Radio Times*.

(*Opposite, top*) Nocturnal serenade.

(*below*) One of Gerard's very few serious paintings, a small water-colour of Hampstead Heath.

September of that same year he took his driving test, the result of which can be deduced from the photograph of him on a bicycle. The entry on 10 December reads: 'Harrow School 2:30' and must have been the day on which he was interviewed for the post of temporary Art Master. At the end of that diary he notes 'School starts 20th Jan. aft. 2:30' and enjoins 'Get a new diary.' Back on 4 April I read 'Lost Gloves' – a tribulation in those days of rationing and clothing coupons and worthy of recording. Apart from this he warns himself of the frequent deadlines to be met for *Lilliput*, the *Tatler*, *Radio Times* and all those magazines he was so happily drawing for then. He regularly noted appointments to have his hair cut and recorded on the end-papers ideas for forthcoming cartoons.

Gerard on a motorised bicycle.

As we approach the time of my appearance on the scene, I should say a little about my background. I was twenty-six when I first met Gerard. As a schoolgirl I had been evacuated from my home town of Folkestone to Merthyr Tydfil in South Wales and later joined the Wrens, spending more than four years in that service. When the war ended I looked around for something to do that involved travelling (a pre-war weekend in Ostend being my only expedition to date). I trained to be a Norland Nurse in order to equip myself for that possibility. After the 18-month course it was necessary to spend a year as a trainee Norlander in a private post in order to complete my qualifications, a condition I viewed as a hindrance to my ambition to travel the five continents of the world. Little did I know that the post I chose was to point me in the direction of Gerard and all that was to stem from our meeting.

In January 1948 I journeyed to Polperro in Cornwall to the home of Rowland Emett and his wife Mary, whose 5-month-old daughter, luckily for me, was in need of care. Towards the latter part of the year I moved to London with the family, and it was during that time that I remember being shown an enchanting invitation received by Rowland and Mary. Written in a spidery hand, covered in candle-wax, and with sealing-wax ladybirds crawling busily in all directions, it was from Gerard Hoffnung, a name unknown to me at the time, inviting them to dine at his home at 5 Thornton Way, London NW11. I thought the letter delightful and charming but heard nothing about the subsequent dinner party and gave it no more thought.

Bidding farewell to the Emetts, I worked in temporary posts on the Continent for about a year until the illness of a mother living

outside Dublin prompted my help in that direction.
Recovery turned out to be speedier than anticipated
and some thought was given to possible venues for her
recuperation. A number of attractive ideas were
discussed, and the thought of going off in mid-winter
in a flying boat to Madeira was one that appealed to
me greatly. I remember my secret disappointment at
the final outcome, to me the least exciting possibility,
which resulted in our journeying to London for a few
weeks' sojourn there.

I was not put out for long. On the second evening
after my arrival I was invited to dinner at the Emetts,
and whether by chance or design, their other guest
turned out to be none other than Gerard Hoffnung.

I remember very clearly the moment of his arrival
that evening. Rowland and I were talking in the sitting
room. There was a discreet tapping and from behind
the door there appeared a round and beaming face,

Annetta shortly before
her meeting with
Gerard.

with an expression at the same time quizzical and almost conspiratorial. His complexion was fresh, his eyes blue, his hair sparse and
his shape portly. I mistakenly judged him to be in his mid-forties,
and in so doing fell into a common error. He was in fact twenty-four
years and ten months old – just nine months younger than myself. I
was immediately fascinated, intrigued and enchanted by this curious
man who kept us entertained with his absurd stories
and mimicries, yet who would suddenly become
intensely serious over matters that concerned
him. I could not help contrasting the
two men – Rowland shy, gentle,
introspective; Gerard
extrovert, ebullient
and robust.

They had become good friends in spite, or perhaps because, of the dissimilarity of their characters.

The evening ended. We took a cab and Gerard dropped me off at my hotel. During the next three weeks we saw each other almost every evening and when the time came for me to leave London, it was apparent that this was an unhappy moment for both of us. I had to return to Ireland for a few more weeks, and Gerard was preparing for his forthcoming visit to the States. Before he left I came over to London for several days to be with him before we bade farewell to each other. He was to be away for several months.

Soon after our meeting he took me to his home in Thornton Way. I clearly remember my first visit. The house reminded me of Miss Havisham's in *Great Expectations*, though in fairness to Marie, there were few, if any, cobwebs to be seen. So much dark panelling only emphasised the fine, frowning furniture, and at first I found the atmosphere sombre – that is, until I was taken upstairs to Gerard's study, where the scene was quite different. In contrast to the rest of the house, this room generated warmth, light and activity. Gerald Priestland once aptly described it as an amalgam of Housemaster's study, Bachelor's den and Alchemist's laboratory. Contained in this room was all the impedimenta of Gerard's everyday life and activities. It was a place for work and his haven for relaxation.

I was to come to know this room very well, and I soon learned how to behave in it. Gerard disliked having his things touched or disturbed. It was important to him that everything was well-ordered, well-cared for and in its rightful place, and it upset him to have it otherwise. Since his reactions were often exaggerated from self-mockery and a love of drama, the explosions when trivial matters irked him would reverberate through the house like some gigantic symphonic crescendo. 'WHERE'S my waste-paper basket? WHY isn't it where it SHOULD be?' he would storm. The commotion would subside quickly when the offending article was restored to him, and peace and tranquillity would return as if it had never been disturbed – Gerard was the least moody of people and not one to bear a grudge. I had been brought up not to indulge my feelings and to believe that one should not give way to anger or temper. On the rare occasions we did, my brother and I were in disgrace, from which state we were only allowed to emerge gradually and with a due sense of the gravity of our misdemeanour. I therefore found Gerard a new and slightly disconcerting experience, but I soon learned to accept and even began to perceive that his reactions were a refreshing, direct way to communicate in contrast to the conventions of my childhood.

5. THORNTON WAY,
LONDON, N.W.11.
SPE. 0789.

This morning after you had said
Adieu to me in your little voice.

But I got your letter just now, and I'm
much happier.

Bless you.

old G.

The only large piece of furniture in the study was a desk, spread at an angle across the bay window, which had belonged to his paternal grandfather. To use the term 'roll-top' would be misleading, for above the roll sat another large drawer and centred above that yet another smaller one. The writing surface was extended to the full, and propped on his closed typewriter was a small flat piece of wood which served as his drawing board. A very old desk lamp directed its light on to his work.

A small round table with two armchairs stood in the centre of the room. On it lay pipes, tobacco jar, ashtray and telephone, his immediate requirements. A welcoming fire burned in the small grate. A Japanese sword lay on the side as a makeshift poker. Somewhere, in a drawer, I still have the ivory handle belonging to it. Bookcases lined much of the wall-space and housed not only his books but also the radio, to which he listened as he worked, and other miscellaneous objects including a dainty diminutive soprano saxophone on which he played some pretty tunes. Dotted around the room lay ocarinas of varying sizes, and I was fascinated by their sweet sound and the way in which Gerard picked up one, then another, and skilfully demonstrated their range and quality.

Ocarina tuition.

Apart from his drawing board which was unimposing, the only other indications of his profession were the jar of large paintbrushes – which I never knew him to use and which stood on the windowsill – and the assorted oddments and paint-pots on the glass shelf over the old-fashioned wash-hand basin which stood nakedly in one corner of the room.

Things were where they were for the sake of convenience, for practical purposes. But in the racks on the shelves above the mantlepiece was an array of pipes of all shapes, sizes and nationalities. I was introduced to some of the more notable ones, a beautiful calabash, a favourite Dunhill, the Peterson he had just bought in Ireland. I handled them with the same reverence Gerard demonstrated as he carefully made his selection and then returned each to its rightful place. With a little tilt this way, a twist that way, he displayed them all to their maximum advantage, finishing the proceedings with a flick of his handkerchief in case any dust should inadvertently have been dislodged during the operation.

Dust there certainly was, particularly over the open fireplace and also because Marie was never allowed to touch the pipes. After her exodus, when her successor had not yet been entrusted with more than attending to the fire, the floor and the waste-paper basket, I would occasionally choose an evening of Gerard's absence from the house. Once he was off to a rehearsal or a prison-visit, I would turn the room out from top to bottom, carefully returning each item to its rightful position, the racks, the pipes, ocarinas, books, sometimes even polishing the trumpet which hung on the door adjoining the

neighbouring room. I have vivid memories of his playing this instrument once to his American publisher during a transatlantic telephone conversation. During these manoeuvres I was always perturbed lest he return home unexpectedly to witness the confusion and upheaval of it all. It was impossible to disguise the result of my efforts, but I noticed he was always delighted with the after-effect and very grateful.

The house itself stood in the centre of Hampstead Garden Suburb, through which, at that time, no public transport ran. The walk to the nearest underground station was pleasant enough, and the time taken varied depending whether I was on my own or with Gerard.

Gerard was an ambler rather than a walker and was easily distracted and brought to a standstill by anything that caught his eye. Cats were the greatest hindrance and, in this vicinity, they abounded. Any neighbourhood cat espied on our journey to Golders Green had to be properly greeted, caressed, conversed with and, in due course, taken leave of. There would be regular pauses to re-light his pipe. I am a fairly brisk walker and confess that I sometimes found these meanderings frustrating and tedious, especially on colder days. Since it was usually I who had persuaded him against taking a taxi, in order to take a little fresh air and exercise instead, I did my best to share his admiration for his feline friends and even to voice my concern for the temperamental behaviour of his pipe. I never did understand why it required so much attention.

Eventually we would reach the bus and underground station in Golders Green. Travelling on public transport was never a dull pastime with Gerard; Gerald Priestland remembers their musical journeys well. Between the two of them, with Gerard's flute-like whistlings and Gerald's humming and singing, they were able to produce, with remarkable dexterity, a convincing rendering of the sounds of an impressive symphony orchestra.

Their performance was, of necessity, muted, with the exception, perhaps of Gerard's occasional loud outbursts at appropriate moments as he expressed the life-like thud of a bass drum or the explosive clash of cymbals. Thus they would pass the time while journeying across London. 'With a few cuts,' recalls Gerry, 'we could manage *The Rite of Spring* between Golders Green and Kensington Church Street.'

When Gerard and I travelled together, I soon learned to avoid, at all costs, being seated opposite him. For there, I was his captive audience, and full advantage would always be taken of this situation. He might decide to roll his eyes alarmingly, to be the sufferer of a nervous tic or perhaps he would stare at me with his eyes very slightly

crossed and a slightly dotty expression on his face. At first I would return his gaze unsmilingly, determined not to encourage his antics and hoping they would cease. Or I would attempt to ignore him altogether. Neither reaction helped, only serving instead to spur him on. The eye-rolling would become rather more energetic, the muscular spasms increasingly obvious, the dotty expression more exaggerated in his attempt to provoke a response from me. At last, I would find I could no longer maintain my resolve to disregard him and, instead, it was all I could do to try my best to stifle my laughter. Having achieved his purpose, Gerard would then fix me with a look of innocent surprise, as if he were mystified by my extraordinary behaviour.

Sybil Shaw, a friend of Gerard's, recalls another journey which took place just after the war on the Paris metro:

Gerard started to tell the story of a pet parrot he had at the time. The details of the story obviously I cannot remember, but the ingenuity and incredible funniness (and the length – it went on for six stations!) of the story had us hysterical with laughter.

But the oddest thing was, that he was getting worried and upset about our laughter. The more we laughed the more serious he got about the parrot. The more he insisted that we must not behave like this in public especially as we were in a foreign country and must have good manners as we were English, *the more uncontrollably we laughed. To this day I don't know whether he was serious about the parrot's adventures or our behaviour.*

Our courtship was protracted. It lasted for very nearly three years and, judging by the number of letters in existence, written while either one or the other of us journeyed across the seas, much of that time was spent in corresponding with each other.

Dearest Giggles, bless you, and bless you again,

P.S. I do . . .
P.P.S. Much . .

T.B.

BEEKMAN
TOWER
ON EXCLUSIVE
BEEKMAN HILL
•
The only hotel
overlooking
New Site
of the
United Nations
and the
East River

3 MITCHELL PLACE (at 49th Street) • NEW YORK 17, N.Y

20th (blimey..),

Annettagram,

           Your letters are getting prettier and prettier
if that is at all possible, and uncle reads them over and
over again, and sometimes he gives a silly chuckle, and
rubs his nosinger with his handkerchiefabus, until it re-
sembles a tomatoling.
I am working vaaaaary hard now, and spend all my time in my
hotel room. Did I tell you that I can also overlook the
river from my window, and it's nice to see all the shipin-
gers pass by, arm in arm. Mighty nice, Yes Sir. Especially
at nightinger when all the lightingers are burning.
Well, I suppose New York is getting more used to me now,
and the noise is still irritating me, but may be not quite as
much. Still I really am a little home sick, and very much
Annettasick, but the time seems to fly past. There is really
no such thing as time, don't you think? I am delighted to
hear that you now have a radio set of your own. If it's not
well why don't you give it an aspirin? I have a radio also
in my room, and it has a television set attached to it. The
latter I ignore, the former I do not Bignore. There is a
programme, one or two programmes in fact, who continually
broadcast good music, all day and all night. The only thing
is that it is often interrupted by hideous advertising which
plays a major part in this country.
I have made great friends with a yankee pussinger. He lives
in the hotel, and he often comes in to my room, and I tell
him about Tim. Enough for to day Sir, I must go back to my
drawing board.

                    A little whisper into one ear,
                    with a cork in the other,

PS I'm all of a giggle.

It was in April 1950, two months after we had met and while I was still working in Ireland that Gerard set off on a long-planned visit to New York to seek his fortune. It was a big step into the unknown, and as the day of departure drew near, the anticipation and suspense became almost unbearable.

He voyaged on the Queen Elizabeth and related his experiences in a letter to me. Gerard found New York exciting, exhilarating, mad and frightening and his letters describe the impact it had on him. New Yorkers in their turn, intrigued by this middle-aged Englishman with his quaintly cherubic air, his mischievousness, wit and humour, lavished upon him their attention and hospitality. He thrived upon audiences and in New York there was no shortage. Sam Wanamaker, the actor and producer who subsequently produced our first Hoffnung concert, described Gerard thus:

We were a good audience and whenever he came to visit us we always assured him of an even bigger audience of friends with whom we wanted to share him. His presence at these gatherings was always a guarantee that our guests would be entertained. Once launched, Gerard's brilliantly observed and recounted stories enchanted and delighted everyone. His wit and humour, nuance and elaboration, his invention and detail combined into a rare comic talent. Whatever other wonderful gifts Gerard had he was at his best as a performer, and I believe, although he would vehemently deny it, that he would rather have succeeded as one than in his own acknowledged profession of cartoonist.

Immediately on his arrival in New York, Gerard set about looking up contacts and showing the contents of his portfolio. Soon he wrote to say that he was doing a series of drawings for a medical magazine. High up in his hotel room, Gerard applied himself seriously to his work. The offer that was to go beyond his wildest expectations came in less than three weeks after his arrival. Fleur Cowles had bought and was editing a new and lavish magazine called *Flair*. She decided she would like Gerard to be her staff cartoonist and promptly engaged him. He would spend six months of each year working in the States. To a young cartoonist of twenty-five this was a staggering opportunity, and he could not believe his good fortune.

'And how is the patient this morning?'.

BEEKMAN
TOWER
ON EXCLUSIVE
BEEKMAN HILL

The only hotel
overlooking
New Site
of the
United Nations
and the
East River

3 MITCHELL PLACE (at 49th Street) • NEW YORK 17, N.Y

16th May.

Dearest Duckie,

It means a great deal to me to get your little letters nearly every day. I sometimes get very lonely here in this big mad city. Especially when I am with a crowd of people, it's not so bad when I am on my own. Can you understand that? When I am alone, at least I can sit in my chair by the window and look at New York, and I can think of you, ducks. What's all this about your going off to South Africa? When and why? Have you had a job offered there? Tell me the news. And if so, how long would you stay there?

I am finding my feet, slowly but surely in this large madhouse. Right now I am working on some Advertising jobs. I have finished making little mental notes at U.N. But nevertheless, I shall have to go back next week. What do you think of my appointment with Flair. I really am very happy about it. Dear Annettinger, I couldn't miss you more than I do. I am really quite fond of you, did I ever tell you that? How is your mother? Give her my regards. And give dear Mrs. Deeny my regards. Have you heard from the Smetts? I wrote to them yesterday. How I hated leaving you at the airport. I love you very much.

T. B.

P.S. I told you that I do.

I have no memory of the South African proposition and evidently did not pursue it as I have never been to that country. Perhaps Gerard's comment in his next letter dissuaded me:

I am a litle sorry about your going off to leave your old uncle. But then it would only be for just about three months, and there is really no such thing as time for us, is there? And besides, if I leave my Auntie A. to go to America, I guess you can leave your uncle for a while. And it will be a wonderful experience for you, duckie. But for heavens sake don't stay there, but then I know you wouldn't. Uncle doesn't like the nasty South Africans with their wicked race prejudices.

On 16 June he describes a terrible experience and its outcome:

I am in a great state of exhaustion. Last night I left my nice, new brief-case in a taxicab. It not only contained my passport, my ticket back to England, all my credentials, some prints which are quite invaluable to me, but also the manuscript (the one and only available) of my children's book, and a sum of 400 dollars, in cash, which I had just collected from the office; my first American salary. At first I was absolutely stunned when I found out, I rushed through the streets like a maniac scrutinising taxicabs; it was two in the morning, when I finally staggered more dead than alive, into a police station, with two dollars in my pocket. The night which followed, was just about the worst I have ever been through. I had hardly any sleep, and was disturbed by horrible nightmares. Annettasplinx, you know, sometimes when one has one particularly ghastly dream, and wakes up in between, one may perhaps say: Thank Heavens, it was only a dream. But here, alas, I dreamed that every half hour the door of my room opened and somebody else gave me back my briefcase. It was a case where the reality was far worse than any bad dream, and where a dream was only a friendly drug, to make one forget.

(*Opposite*) Gerard in New York.

An emergency operation: 'On your marks . . .'.

This morning I rushed around in a frenzy, I rang many telephone numbers, lost property offices, police stations, only to be disappointed again and again. It was awful, you have no idea how awful. I sat in my office at Flair *near a breakdown, and I am not exaggerating. Everybody was very kind, I had only one wish, to put my head onto your knee and weep. Forgive this stupid confession, but that was how I felt. At three o'clock, one of the girls at the office rushed in with the overwhelming news: The case had been found by the driver, and returned to the police. At four o'clock it was mine once more, and nothing was missing, it was all there just as I left it. This sudden change of emotion, the swing from utter hopelessness to the joyful reality was too much for your old Pollinger, he just about collapsed and then he slept, Aye, slept like a babynger, sweetly and soundly until this hour: it's ten o'clock. I am still pretty exhausted though, but tomorrow, I shall be all right, I know it.*

For the rest of his stay until the end of July he spent most of his time hard at work. In his letters to me he always mentions the lone-

liness he suffered in New York, and he sometimes spoke of it much later on when recalling his time there:
Tonight I am overcome by a great feeling of emptiness inside of me, which depresses me much. I do not know why this is so, but I dare say the terrible heat is partly responsible. Also the air-conditioned offices, with their artificial draughts, have left me with an attack of rheumatism which is not very funny; I am hardly able to move my shoulder or head. And then, of course, everyone went away over the holidays and I have been in the office on my own. That is awful, it sometimes happens. The place is so huge, and makes me feel such a worm. True enough in one way I am satisfied: I have done a lot of work, and the work has made me feel good. You know how it is when one has just finished a good job of work, possibly the highest degree of satisfaction. Jes, old dear, the work is all that keeps your uncle together just lately. I don't know what has happened to me. I am an absolute bundle of nerves; perhaps I have been overworking, perhaps this mad place does not agree with me. I am so looking forward to getting back. This strain, this dreadful being lonely all the time, is a bad thing. I must get back. The work has not been influenced by my troubles, I'm glad to say. As I wrote to you in my last letter, I have turned out some of my best drawings, while in New York.

Towards the end of July he packed his bags and returned home across the Atlantic. Seven or eight months after his return he was to be deeply disappointed by news of the sudden collapse of *Flair* in New York; it was entirely unexpected. The lavish and sophisticated magazine, owned by Cowles Publications, had all the indications of a solid, stable enterprise, and Gerard could not believe that such a thing had happened. It expunged in a flash the hard work he had put into his months in New York and his plans to return there in the near future. It was a bitter blow.

Fortunately there was too much going on in London for it to be more than a momentary setback and nothing could detract from the success he had achieved during his time over there.

Gerard settled down to work again. For *Saturday Evening Post* in the USA he illustrated several poems by Ogden Nash. He started on his illustrations to Ravel's *L'Enfant et les Sortilèges*. This opera was one his mother sang to him as a child, and he knew it well and loved it dearly. When he had finished the paintings, which he did for his own pleasure, he took them over to Paris to show to Colette, who had written the libretto. She was then an old lady and she was so delighted with his work that she wrote a special caption for each one of the fourteen paintings. Gerard was overjoyed at her reaction and envisaged a children's book with a special appeal for adults. Various

(*Overleaf*) Gerard's impression of the United Nations, his first drawing published in *Flair*.

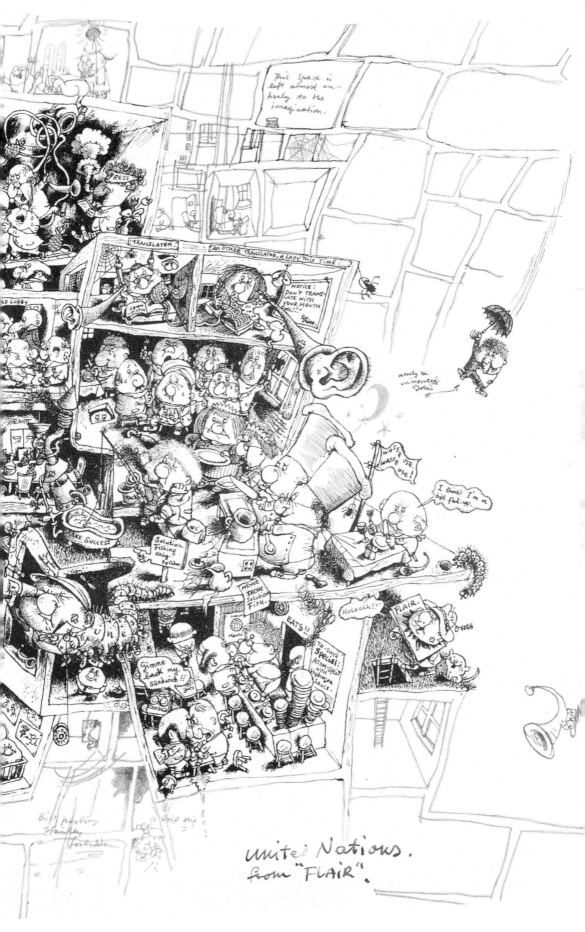

publishers mulled over the idea and turned it down (mostly for reasons of cost, for the work was in full colour). After a year or two Gerard became discontented with the paintings. His style had been modified in that very short time and had become far less grotesque. He no longer drew the bulbous gnome-like little creatures that up till then had filled his pages to overflowing. He felt particularly critical of the way in which he had exaggerated the size of the boy's head and caricatured his face. He decided to re-do the illustrations entirely. Sadly this idea was not to be fulfilled and we are left with his first endeavour.

For a while I adhered to Gerard's decision at the time that the paintings should not be published. But after several years as I encountered the delight people expressed when they saw them, I changed my mind. Along with Colette's captions and a translation by Christopher Fry, they were published in a book entitled *The Boy and the Magic*.

There is a strange and unsolved mystery as to the whereabouts of two of the paintings used in the book. In 1951 during the Festival of Britain they were exhibited in the foyer of the then brand-new Fes-

tival Hall. On their return home they were hung for a short time on our staircase until Gerard began to feel dissatisfaction with them. At this point they were removed from their frames and, still in their mounts, placed in the steel filing cabinet in Gerard's study where they remained till after his death. When I came later to look at them, only twelve of the fourteen paintings were there, with no indication of the whereabouts of the two that were missing. Their absence remains inexplicable. It is possible that Gerard sent a couple of them away to be exhibited somewhere, but I worked very closely with him and would have been aware of this. There is no correspondence to this effect in the files either. Perhaps he destroyed them. This is unlikely too since one of the missing paintings was the first in the series, depicting the boy writing at his table in the nursery; Gerard criticised it the least and considered it his favourite. The other was of the old armchair dancing with the pretty little French Bergère.

It was a sore loss. The only record that exists of the collection is a set of very poor quality colour positives taken at a time when *Life* magazine was interested in publishing the series – better than nothing, but very unsatisfactory material for printers to work from.

Gerard's career continued to gather momentum. A talk submitted to the BBC in 1950 was accepted and marked his first public success

(*Left and above*) Two paintings from the opera *L'Enfant et les Sortilèges* from *The Boy and the Magic*.

as a raconteur. Entitled 'Fungi on Toast', it was subsequently published in *The Listener*, his first contact with his listening public.

At much the same time a chance meeting with Ian Messiter was to establish him on the air. Precariously perched on a high ladder drawing a large mural for the 1950 BBC Exhibition, Gerard got into conversation with this young BBC Producer who was admiring his drawing. Ian was the inventor of *One Minute Please* (a radio programme which, after more than forty years, is still continuing under the title of *Just a Minute*). So struck was he by the idiosyncracy of his manner that Ian asked Gerard to take part in the programme. Members of the two panels included Frank Muir, Dennis Norden, Kenneth Horne, the beloved actress and comedienne, Yvonne Arnaud, and the controversial Gilbert Harding. Gerard's imagination sparkled as he held forth for one minute on a given subject without pausing and without repeating himself. Bruno Adler wrote:

So began a new phase, which was not confined only to drawing. The radio revealed him as a natural comedian, both in his talks and in his activity as a member of the quiz programme One Minute Please. *These really brought him the wide popularity which turned him into a national personality. What he said and the way he said it were just as oddly absurd as his drawings, turning logic inside out and reason upside down. It was not unlike Lewis Carroll, and his way of doing it only added to*

A mural for the BBC exhibition, 1950.

the fun. He would produce some harmless little anecdote which immediately set his audience off in fits of laughter. It was really extraordinary, since he used none of the tricks of the professional comedian. And these talks were often entirely improvised, unlike his drawings, which were the result of careful thought and tireless concentration down to the very smallest detail.

Another favourite series was a radio programme called *Saturday Night on the Light* on which he was interviewed each week on a variety of subjects by Charles Richardson. As these broadcasts were entirely spontaneous, some were more hilarious than others. I particularly like one on the topic of sport, not Gerard's favourite indulgence, in which Charles asked Gerard, 'Do you swim?' 'Yes, I swim.' 'Where do you swim?' 'I swim in the water.' Charles, more irately, 'Yes, yes, but where do you swim, in pools?' 'Yes, I swim in pools, that is correct, there's more room.'

It was after Gerard's return from America that, with some slight trepidation, I first took him down to my home in Folkestone. I was naturally concerned that the three people most dear to me should be happy with each other. (Gerard afterwards became very fond of my brother, Tony, who was working in Burma at this time; the two did not meet up properly until later on.) I have a great admiration for my parents and the calm, almost matter-of-fact way in which they ac-

cepted Gerard. He was a most singular person. Equally I am grateful to him for his part in making a success of the relationship. It helped that my father was a sweet and gentle man, shy and reserved, not without his own quiet sense of humour. Gerard quickly labelled him an introvert and would mischeviously tease him and pull his leg. Would he walk down the road without his trousers on for £1000, I once heard him ask my father (who rarely chose even to appear outside his bedroom in a dressing gown) – implying that Gerard himself would be happy to do it for nothing. After what had happened the previous evening, nothing came as a surprise. He and Gerard were strolling in the garden and I, helping my mother prepare the evening meal, chanced to glance out of the kitchen window. There was a most curious sight. Gerard, I saw, had clasped my father around the legs, and having lifted him several inches off the ground was then, very gently, returning him to a standing position. The odd thing was that neither appeared to find this behaviour at all unusual. I learned later that Gerard, fascinated by my father's height and slenderness had first asked his permission before testing out his weight. Three of the birthday cards he sent, express better than my words Gerard's affection and fondness for his father-in-law.

My mother, more robust, tolerated Gerard's eccentricities, but would stand no nonsense when she considered his behaviour too boisterous or obstreperous. Once when we were all on our way to the sea in the car, my mother pointed out my old school to Gerard, little realising the effect this information would have on him. Stopping the car, and clad only in his swimming shorts and sun hat, he alighted and made several deep obeisances towards the school that had educated his wife. It was really ridiculous. Even my mother was almost speechless on that occasion. All she managed was, 'Gerard, get back into the car at once, you are not properly dressed,' as if his behaviour in other respects had been perfectly normal.

Learning that Gerard's thinning hair caused him discomfort from being cold in bed at night, my mother, who was always concerned for his well-being, knitted him a handsome bed-hat, complete with tassel. He wrote a charming letter of thanks which delighted her. On the next visit to my home, as the taxi reached the gate of the house Gerard quickly delved into his pocket and, to my great surprise, produced and donned his nightcap. I doubt if my mother was seriously convinced that he had worn it for the whole of the journey, but it was the funniest sight as he greeted her in his overcoat and scarf with her creation on top of his head. Certainly it made the taxi-driver's day. The hat was put to frequent use on

Happy Birthday to our Daddy Longlegs.

Happy @Birthdayss to our dear Percy
from Annetta and Gerard.

winter's nights and later, following serious discussions on variations in shape, design and colour, an even better one was knitted for him.

The effect Gerard had on my home was typical of the way in which his presence affected so many people. My parents had lived in Folkestone for most of their regulated, quiet lives. The advent of Gerard changed them. I would see my father bubbling and chuckling in a way that I had rarely witnessed before. My mother secretly delighted in all he did. They derived enormous pleasure from his published drawings and his broadcasts, as if they absorbed the warmth and enthusiasm he exuded. They adored him. When Gerard died, my knowledge of their profound sense of loss was an added grief.

Soon after we met, Gerard had confessed to me his love for a particular musical instrument, the tuba. It attracted him both aurally and visually, and it seemed unlikely that he could live much longer without actually possessing one.

The momentous decision was taken. We met at our usual trysting place in Piccadilly. Whenever I reached there first, I would listen as well as watch out for Gerard. Our signature tune (more his than mine, since I was never able to whistle with such strength and verve) was the opening few bars of Bartok's Second Piano Concerto. Above the roar of the traffic I would hear the melody waft towards me before I saw him, and there he would be. On this particular afternoon I detected an air of expectancy and excitement, even of urgency as we greeted each other. 'I thought we might go and look at some tubas this afternoon,' he said.

The new knitted night AND nose-hat.
(pure wool)

Tilly, as she became known, was a B flat bombardon and was sitting in the window of Boosey and Hawkes music shop.

She was selected, after careful and lengthy deliberation, from all the other tubas inside the shop. The cheque was signed, and she was ours. Gerard carried her from the shop in his arms, and we walked across Piccadilly to a restaurant in Jermyn Street. The excitement had given Gerard an appetite. We must have appeared a curious trio as we sat at the table, the tuba occupying the third chair. We travelled home by taxi and laid the household's latest acquisition on the kitchen table. For the next three hours we cleaned and polished her, gingerly removing her valves, washing her mouthpiece and generally getting to know the intricacies of her plumbing. If I felt a little put out at being confronted with such a mammoth and dirty job on my precious time off (cleaning a tuba is like painting the Forth Bridge – it goes on and on) this was made up for by Gerard's enthusiasm and delight, which knew no bounds. Finally, transformed by our endeavours, she lay there radiant, resplendent and magnificent,

glowing shiny and silver, a veritable beauty of an instrument. Exhausted, we made ourselves a cup of tea and sat there for a long time admiring her.

Dear me! How different was the atmosphere next day when I received a telephone call from Gerard. The temperature of the previous day's euphoria had plummeted. Doubts and misgivings had replaced his confidence and optimism. Poor Gerard. A morning spent trying to play his new treasure had left him frustrated and unsettled. 'It sounds more like an elephant in pain' he said, crestfallen and disgruntled. Marie's objections to the sounds coming from his room added insult to injury. Had he not acted frivolously without careful thought, he asked me? Spent too much money? Should he not take her back to Boosey and Hawkes and forget all about it? Would he ever be able to play the thing? There were very few superficial worries of Gerard's that could not be assuaged with a good meal. By the end of the repast he had reached the conclusion that it was all right on occasions to pander to a whim, that the £20 paid (much money in those days) could be thought of in terms of an investment, that Boosey and Hawkes would probably not be too happy to be asked to take Tilly back, and that he should have a few lessons before prejudging his performance on the instrument.

As Gerard became more ambitious, he was able to throw off longer and more complicated passages of music, and the thought that he might one day soon play in an orchestra became uppermost in his mind. To prepare for such an eventuality he borrowed a second instrument so that now there were two tubas lying on his sofa. The visitor, unlike Tilly, was an orchestral tuba pitched in 'F' and hard to come by in those days. (Later on, in 1955, Boosey and Hawkes made for Gerard the first 'F' tuba manufactured by their company in thirty years.)

Soon after this he journeyed forth to keep a very important appointment, an audition for the position of tuba player in the Ernest Read Junior Orchestra, where he met with a slight setback. 'Everyone in my orchestra has to read music,' said Ernie to Gerard who, having thrown off with admirable virtuosity several well-known themes, (albeit not all of them written for tuba since one of them was definitely the horn virtuoso melody from *Till Eulenspiegel*) was defeated by a request to do some sight reading. 'You'd better go away and learn and come back next week,' Ernie added with a twinkle in his eye.

This Gerard did and was installed into the brass section of the orchestra. By dint of much preparation, by procuring his part well in advance, and with the help and support of the trombone section on his left, he managed somehow to count his bars and to render a good account of himself. Later he progressed and joined Morley College Orchestra, whose conductor Lawrence Leonard remembers Gerard's early days with the orchestra:

During the first few months of his position as regular tuba player with our orchestra – for it was inconceivable even after just one rehearsal that he should not be our regular tuba player – he found his way round some of the most difficult pieces in the repertoire, including The Rite of Spring *and Shostakovitch's 10th Symphony. He did this by a combination of sound instinct and natural genius, for his experience was certainly not equal to it.*

Ernest Read insisted that Gerard learn to read music before he took him on as tuba player in his orchestra.

He also became in a short while our vice president, our official conscience, our court jester and our own personal volcano. Although no-one could accuse the Morley Orchestra of exactly neglecting new music, our efforts were futile as far as Gerard was concerned. 'The Glow-worm Orchestra,' he would comment bitterly. 'No initiative, no excitement, no new works. I know a piece. Heard it this morning from Brussels. Jolivet. That's what we want – Jolivet.'

Ever intent on improving his sight reading, Gerard started taking piano lessons from an excellent teacher, the mother of our good friend Michael Flanders. Michael remembered his mother claiming Gerard to be the most exasperating pupil she had ever taught. His enquiring mind frequently enlivened any demands made on his concentration with his own improvisations in the style of Ravel, or with experiments in playing with the elbows while seated on the floor. One big distraction at the Flanders house was their splendid cat George (a close friend and ally of Gerard's) and another could have been the sound of Michael and Donald (Swann) working together on the songs for the first of their very successful shows, *At the Drop of a Hat*. At our first Christmas party, all present were given a foretaste of those wonderful and brilliantly witty songs.

Howard Ferguson, the composer and a neighbour of Gerard's at that time, also recalls early efforts to play the tuba:

What surprised me almost more than Gerard's ability as a whistler was my discovery that he was unable at that time to read music. Having heard him quote so many contemporary works with absolute accuracy and dash off brilliant passages on his tiny saxophone or on one of his many ocarinas, it never occurred to me that all this might perhaps be

done by ear. Yet when I once offered him a score with which to follow a broadcast, he slowly answered, 'But my dear fel-low, I can't read the thing.'

Later, when he had succumbed to his longing to possess a tuba, he painstakingly learnt his notes by ploughing through a Tutor; for he was determined to fit himself to play in an orchestra. But it was hard going. Every now and again he would appear on my doorstep, tuba tucked under his arm, with an apology for the interruption and the heart-melting request, 'How-ard, could you just make sure I've got this right? I think I can manage the flats, but the sharps are im-poss-ible.' (Rests were also a bit of a problem.) He would then follow me into the house, sit down in front of a music stand and blow his way through a move-ment of Tchaikovsky's Symphony Pathetique.

There is a lovely story of what happened to Gerard when he was suddenly, as an emergency measure, called upon by Lawrence Leonard to collect Aaron Copland from the Cavendish Hotel in Jermyn Street and take him to a rehearsal of the Morley College Orchestra that he had kindly agreed to conduct.

At that time we had just acquired our first motor car, a tiny 1934

Austin 10 with the apt registration number of BEL 790. Beige in colour, dignified, sedate, complete with leather seats and sun roof, her appearance belied her age. We were proud owners. With space for two of us in the front and for the tuba at the rear, what more could we want?

Outside the Cavendish Hotel Gerard took the opportunity to park in the small vacant space between a Rolls-Royce and a Bentley. It is understandable, I suppose, that Copland, coming out of the hotel with Gerard should make first for one and then the other of these limousines. He wavered uncertainly as he was guided to what must have looked like a child's dinky toy. He hesitated, glancing at it speculatively before summoning his courage and getting in. The fact that I had been shopping that morning for toilet rolls, kitchen towels and a variety of household items all strewn across the back seat around the tuba could not have helped to allay his misgivings. Gerard was also by this time a little nervous. He had not long passed his driving test, and getting out of the small space proved more dif-ficult than entering it had been. Gears were crashed and several short sharp lurches shook the car as it leapt into motion. I am sure that the two of them conversed reasonably during the journey, and certainly the following week Aaron was sufficiently recovered to come out to Thornton Way for dinner one evening. But when-ever Gerard told this story he always maintained that his passenger reached Morley College and extricated himself from the car with great relief, and that when, at the start of the rehearsal, he recognised the face behind the tuba, he very nearly fell off the rostrum with fright.

It was soon after I met Gerard that I real-ised he was the person with whom I wanted to spend the rest of my life. I loved him dearly

Aaron Copland.

and, indeed he loved me. But whereas I was prepared to devote my life to him, he did not find the prospect of marriage an engaging one. It made him uneasy, and he feared the limitations, the restrictions and the responsibilities his lively mind imagined it would surely impose upon him – and his career. My plan of action after more than two years' devotion to Gerard was not prompted solely in order to sort Gerard out. Early in our relationship I had mentioned to him that I was thinking of becoming an air hostess (at that time a sought-after occupation) and I was surprised how much my remark upset him. It had never been my intention to make Norland Nursing a lifetime's career and I was serious in my resolve to train as an air hostess. Perhaps, too, it was a small assertion of independence. I was certainly keen to branch out into some new activity. The fact that Gerard feared the thought of flying was fortuitous and for me, it transpired, a piece of great good fortune. As I progressed success-fully from one interview to the next he became increasingly sub-dued. When I was finally accepted and the date for the commence-ment of my training fixed, he could stand the situation no longer. 'How can I possibly get on with my work with the thought of you flying about up there in the air? It's alarming and disquieting,' he lamented.

Marriage suddenly seemed less alarming and he happily accepted the idea of losing his bachelor state. We never regretted the decision.

We were married in Folkestone register office on a wet and windy
day in November 1952. There followed a reception in the Queen's
Hotel (which has long since been pulled down) where our wedding
cake was high-lighted by the model of a tuba sitting on its top tier.
This replica had been very cleverly designed and modelled by my
mother's dentist! A long-standing admirer of Gerard's, Mr Wren had
been intrigued by the prospect of his becoming one of our family
and had asked if he might make this contribution towards the occasion. It was constructed from the substance from which the gums of
false teeth are made, then carefully silvered, and fortunately bore no
resemblance to dental technology.

After our departure we hurried up to London and took part in the
Saturday evening programme *In Town Tonight*. It was broadcast live
but, as was the practice in those days, the entire interview was
scripted. We had even been required to attend a rehearsal the previous week so that we could practise our parts! I have a recording of
the broadcast. It sounds dated and dreadfully stilted, but is a happy
reminder of that time.

Our honeymoon was spent in Farringford on the Isle of Wight in a lovely old hotel that had previously been the home of Alfred Lord Tennyson. We took long walks exploring coast and countryside and getting blown off our feet, returning to sit by roaring fires. After a week it was back to London and the drawing board for Gerard, and for me the start of a very new existence.

My first model.

Alongside all this, other important events had been taking place in 1952. Gerard's first book had been published. He had illustrated a text by an American writer, James Broughton, whom he had met in New York. Entitled *The Right Playmate*, it was published in the United States by Farrar Strauss and Young and in the United Kingdom by Rupert Hart-Davis. A tongue-in-cheek story of a young boy's search for the right playmate, the book created a stir on publication, but in time it drifted into obscurity.

'En francais'.

The publication of his first drawing in *Punch* gave him keen pleasure. Gerard became a regular contributor to *Punch*, though not all the drawings he submitted were published. 'Not quite!' the art editor, Russell Brockbank, would write on the rejection slip. Sometimes it was 'Not *quite*' and once '*Nearly*, but not quite.' It made no difference. It was always a disappointment to have a drawing rejected. Later he was asked to do a cover for the magazine. I

First drawing published in *Punch*, *Hoffnung's Harlequinade*.

remember that this particular drawing caused him immense difficulty and trouble, and he made three complete attempts before the final one was to his satisfaction. It took well over a week and a number of really good meals to keep him going.

A sad tale: sometime in the mid-sixties I allowed ten of these original drawings to become part of a *Punch* exhibition on tour to Europe for a year. On its return to this country the warehouse where the whole exhibition was stored caught fire and all was lost in the blaze. Despondent at the loss of the drawings, I determined that some good should come from their destruction. With the insurance compensation I took my children on a skiing holiday and we thoroughly enjoyed this unexpected bonus.

After our marriage I soon learned that I had to share Gerard's love not only with his tuba, but also with his cat. Gerard was devoted to all cats, in particular to Tim, the heldentenor of the neighbourhood – who would absent himself from home

A 'Not *quite*' drawing rejected by *Punch*.

(*Above*) a drawing from
The Isle Of Cats, Scolar Press.

sometimes for days, returning (to the vast relief of Marie and Gerard)
battered and scarred like some decrepit old warrior. Even I, not especially a cat lover, formed an admiration for his stoicism and shared
in the sorrow when he died a few years later.

Gerard's fascination with cats had already been apparent when he
was at Highgate School. There, it is reported, he was frequently to
be found visiting the kitchen staff and impressing upon them the
beauty and virtue of the latest batch of kittens threatened by his
mother with expulsion from home. The school accepted the bestowal
of several such offerings and a Hoffnung line of descent was
established.

So deep was Gerard's love of cats and so intense his powers of
observation that he had an uncanny ability to imitate them. I remember vividly one day when, feeling guilty over some wickedness or
other which he had perpetrated, he came to me to seek forgiveness.
He came on all fours mimicking the movements of a cat, winding
himself around my legs with such persistence and rubbing his head
against me with such affectionate perseverance that I had the uncanny feeling he really was a cat. It was a combination of acting and
clowning which held me spellbound for a few moments before I collapsed in a heap of laughter. If the maxim 'Laugh and grow fat' were

true, I should have been very plump at that time, so often was I con-
vulsed with laughter.

There is a curious story, something that happened to the Messiters
who came to live in the neighbourhood after Gerard's death. Neither
Ian nor Enid were particularly interested in cats, but arriving home
one cold mid-evening, they found a large black cat on their front
doorstep who welcomed them with a friendliness, warmth and affection they found impossible to ignore. So taken were they by this
behaviour they made no effort to dissuade the creature from his obvious determination to join them indoors. Whereupon he settled
himself in front of the fire, washed himself carefully and promptly
fell asleep. Awakening after an hour, he stretched, arose and made
clear his intention to depart. It was only then that a small disc was
discovered hanging from his collar. On it was written the address of
the house where Gerard and I had lived in Thornton Way. To this
day, Ian is convinced that it was Gerard returned to say hallo. I have
never had such a visitation and only once have I dreamed of Gerard.
I was waiting in Piccadilly Circus when his face appeared in the
crowd. He gave me a warm conspiratorial smile and I woke with a
glow of happiness.

I do, however, have my own cat story which Gerard would have
loved. I was tidying my front garden when a young man from a
nearby house strolled by. I had recently had letters published in the
press asking for any Hoffnung reminiscences that might be included

in this book, and from one of these letters he had discovered the fact that I was a neighbour of his. We talked, and he explained that he had always been a great admirer of Gerard's work. As he paused to leave he said, 'By the way, your little black cat is a frequent visitor to our house. At first, when I read the name and address on his collar I used to think "Hoffnung! What a lovely name to call a cat." It was only after I read your letter in the newspaper that I realised that he was a real Hoffnung.' (Her name was Phoebe!)

I have selected my favourite cat drawings from the many that exist. Included are some illustrations to a children's book by John Symonds entitled *The Isle of Cats* – the pictures hanging on the wall of the art gallery are worth scrutiny (*see* pages 114–15).

(*Above*) a drawing from the *Isle of Cats*. Scolar Press.

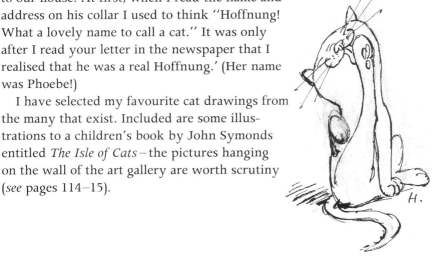

Dropcloth for Sean O'Casey's play, *Purple Dust*.

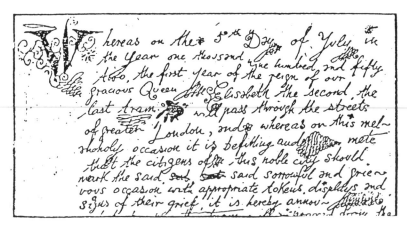

Whereas on the 5th Day of July in the Year one thousand nine hundred and fifty Also, the first year of the reign of our gracious Queen Elisabeth the Second, the last tram will pass through the streets of greater London, and whereas on this melancholy occasion it is befitting and mete that the citizens of this noble city should mark the said said sorrowful and grievous occasion with appropriate tokens, displays and signs of their grief, it is hereby announced

In between his more serious work at the drawing board, a variety of demands were made on Gerard's time. A ticket to be designed for a special occasion, a farewell journey on the last tram to run in London, a documentary to be narrated describing the life and habits of the naked mole-rat – this last at a request of the Wellcome Foundation. An exciting collaboration with Sam Wanamaker involved Gerard in the design of a front drop-cloth for the theatre production of Sean O'Casey's play *Purple Dust*. This was a combination of poetry, music, farce and Irish blarney, and the setting was the interior of a dilapidated Irish castle. Gerard's excitement ran high as he worked on his first theatrical project, and particularly when he saw his design magnified at least one hundred and fifty times. Alas, the whereabouts of the drop-cloth is unknown, if, indeed, it still exists anywhere at all; but Gerard's original design is reproduced here along with a copy of a short correspondence that took place between Mr Hoffnung and Mr Wanamaker.

All the time it seemed that the tuba played an increasingly important part in our lives – we are shown actually living in one on our

SAM WANAMAKER, ESQ.,
31, ABBEY LODGE, N.2.
PARK ROAD,
LONDON, N.W.8.

To be delivered by hearse if possible.

first Christmas card. Gerard appeared with it on television, wrote articles about it, would discuss it at the slightest provocation, and often regaled his guests, trapped at the dinner table, with his latest show-piece. In times of stress it was a solace to him. 'I must just have a little blow' was a phrase often heard in those days when ideas would not come or tedious things were happening around him.

Serious practising always took place on the landing half-way up the stairs, where Gerard discovered acoustics most pleasing to his ear. It was not a habit guaranteed to encourage smooth running of the household, for the landing was not big and invariably one was trapped up or downstairs for this period of time. At least the situation, when it existed, was apparent to all within earshot. And my musical education, so sorely neglected before I met Gerard, was interestingly (if a little lopsidedly) enriched as I became more and more familiar with the tuba parts of the modern concert repertoire of that time.

At first when we went abroad there was a problem, for the instrument was too cumbersome to take with us. Not surprisingly, Gerard soon contrived tactics to temper the sometimes acute withdrawal symptoms he suffered on these occasions. Whereas some people seek out a cathedral, an art gallery or perhaps a museum when visiting a place for the first time, Gerard would make straight for the local music shop. There he would sit and discuss the characteristics of the native tubas and with any luck be allowed to try one out for a little while.

Shortly after we returned from one of these trips abroad he wrote a letter to his friend Ian Messiter:
I am delighted that you went, now that you are coming back. We will

have a magnificent celebration at No 5 . . . and I will spice the occasion with a song on the tuba. I have learnt a lot on this instrument since you left us, its tone is truly like a nightingale now.

But let me tell you of the interesting time I had in Germany. I brought back with me a new tuba my dear boy. It is quite the largest tuba you have seen. Unfortunately every time I blow it I am so exhausted I have to lie down for half an hour.

I had to give it a bunk to itself it is so big, and the customs made me play it to prove it was my own instrument. I gave them my entire repertoire and the train was held up for twenty minutes but I didn't have to pay a single sixpence duty on it, what do you think of that?

Soon after we were married, Gerard decided it was time I learned to play a musical instrument. It seemed the normal sequence of events that he should produce a magnificent trombone. He watched expectantly for my reaction of pleasure. I did not disappoint

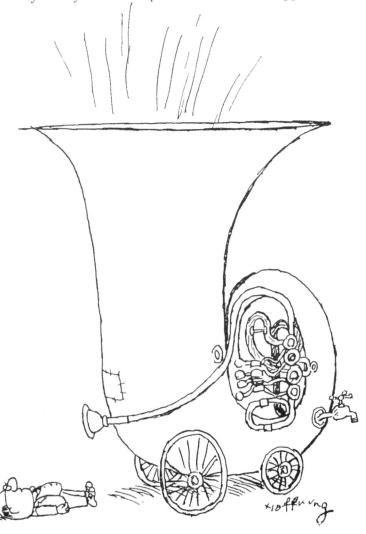

him – how could I – so eager was he that we should make music together. Alas, it soon became obvious that trombone-playing was not my forte. As I sat, door and windows closed, in the sitting room, practising my long notes and making unpleasant sounds, my lips became numbed and I increasingly disillusioned. My talents, had I any, quite obviously lay in other directions and, as his mother had done when Gerard gave up the violin, Gerard had to accept the fact that we were not to become a duo.

Advertisements were another outlet in which he could express his love for the tuba. In the 1952 Christmas issue of the Ford Motor Company's house magazine he concocted a charming scene. Embellished on the bell of the magnificent bombardon are the words Ford Excelsior Sonorous, and sitting facing the performer are three new models introduced at that time by Ford, the Zephyr, the Zodiac and the Consul.

Another time, for Simmonds Contents Gauges and the slogan 'Does the gauge measure up to its job?,' the tuba took on a truly original role. And in a memento for our friends, Gerald and Sylvia Priestland, just then off to the States, Gerard draws himself clutching his own brass model in 'F'.

Unaware of its significance, he also started to draw the little figure of a conductor exaggeratedly expressing a variety of orchestral moods. 'They might make a book,' he mused as the number of Maestros increased beyond the likelihood of acceptance by a magazine or periodical. Several publishers thought not; but one did, and there began a collaboration with the firm of Dobson Books which was to last for thirty years and only ended with Dennis Dobson's own death and the events that succeeded it.

The little book, *The Maestro*, published in 1953, sold out rapidly on publication and has been reprinted countless times. It was the first of a series of six musical-cartoon books (now all published by Souvenir Press) which Gerard produced with almost yearly regularity. They are irrepressible and have remained bestsellers throughout the world, even turning up one day in a Russian magazine.

William Mann wrote:

Of all Gerard Hoffnung's gifts the musical one was the most individual, when applied in context to the rest of the man. It was not that he was a musical genius; his musical gift was a flair. But when his draughtsman's eye played upon music, it did so upon an art which he knew from

Знакомьтесь—Джерард Хоффнунг!

НЕ ПРАВДА ЛИ, ЗАБАВНЫЙ АВТОГРАФ? Таким рисунком обычно открывал свои сборники музыкальных карикатур английский художник Джерард [ ] Имя его очень популярно в Англии. О художнике говорят как о добром приятеле: «А-а, Хоффнунг! Чудак и острослов, фанатик музыки, который всех уверял, что в детстве ему по ошибке дали карандаш вместо смычка...»

Разноцветные, карманного формата книжечки «Симфонический оркестр Хоффнунга» я видел в руках у многих слушателей на концертах, которые мне удалось посетить во время поездки в Англию. Разглядывая рисунки, люди всегда улыбались. В их возвышенную любовь к музыке художник вносил смешливые, озорные нотки. Он находил неожиданные ассоциации различным инструментам оркестра: струны арфы — спицы старинного велосипеда, раскрытый рояль — будуар со всеми принадлежностями женской косметики, на длинном корпусе басовой флейты сушится белье, литаврист прослушивает докторским стетоскопом отслужившие свой век литавры и т. д.

Это типично английский юмор: внешне все очень серьезно, деловито, и смех рождается именно от такой вот практичности взгляда на вещи.

Джерард Хоффнунг родился в 1925 году. Учился в Хайгетской школе живописи, работал иллюстратором во многих английских газетах и журналах. Он был инициатором музыкальных фестивалей, смотров; был вице-президентом симфонического оркестра колледжа Морли, где даже играл на... басовой тубе!

Хоффнунг умер молодым, не прожив и 35 лет. В честь него в Лондоне каждый год проходят популярные Хоффнунг-фестивали.

А. Медведев

Двойной концерт для одной скрипки.

Фортепиано (Большой будуар).

Техника безопасности тромбониста.

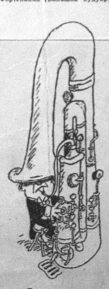

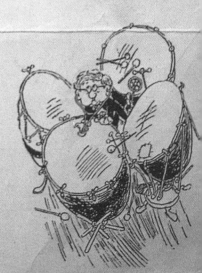

Арфа (А почему бы и нет?)

Пульт управления контрафаготом.

Внимание и забота — прежде всего!

Gerard at a book fair.

These seven drawings from *The Hoffnung Symphony Orchestra*, Souvenir Press, were reproduced in a Russian magazine.

the inside. There have been many cartoonists of genius, but none of them, I think, has known music so intimately and loved it so deeply, and thereby revealed so much about it through the medium of drawing and painting. Hoffnung drew about music as a connoisseur of the art of listening, and as a knowledgeable musical executant. Music is a territory with its own language and laws and habits. To the foreigner they appear so much gibberish and mumbo-jumbo, but Gerard Hoffnung was no foreigner to that territory; he had lived there long enough to qualify for naturalisation.

He was not, however, a professional musician. Hoffnung played solos in public, at concerts and on television, and he knew something of the private emotions of the musician in the public's gaze. But he remained an amateur of the most ardent and accomplished sort, and so, although he was quick to perceive and lampoon the vanity and pretentiousness of the solo performer his art was entirely innocent of the bitterness and cynicism which sometimes assail the professional musician. He drew music not as a nagging, possessive and slightly ageing spouse, but as a young and beautiful 'inamorata' whose amusing foibles only enhanced the love he felt for her. He would tease her sometimes, not out of cruelty, but in order to remind himself and others that the greatest musicians are a little lower than the angels, and that achievement is best measured by the standards of the unattainable.

The most primitive form of joke about music is the direct caricature, *and the first of Hoffnung's books of musical drawings is simply a set of caricatures, developed from the famous strip-cartoon by Wilhelm Busch about a virtuoso pianist.* The Maestro *adapts Busch's method to the conductor (no conductor in particular, I think) simply exaggerating the gestures by which the most demonstrative of the breed convey the changing moods of a scrupulously marked score. In retrospect* The Maestro *seems like a naive, as yet unripened, blueprint for the brilliant and far-reaching caricature that was to be the 'Concerto for Conductor and Orchestra', which Hoffnung himself performed at his Interplanetary Music Festival in 1958; at the time the charm and good humour of the book were quickly recognised, except by those who regarded music as no laughing matter.*

Hoffnung's acumen as a caricaturist quickly ripened. The jokes in his second book, The Hoffnung Symphony Orchestra, *involved a good deal more imagination; many of them explore what was to be a fertile source of musical humour, the resemblance of the musical instruments to other articles in daily life—the simile in fact. Hoffnung's visual similes are generally domesticated—the boudoir grand piano complete with looking-glass, scent bottles and trinket drawers, and the contrabassoon with fitted drainpipe and drain—as if to suggest, what laymen are surprised to discover, that the musician is at heart a domestic animal, prone to accidents— particularly if he is a percussionist—fond of beer and cups of tea which he brews in his timpani. But often Hoffnung's similes are drawn from animal life: the castanets are oysters, the saxophone's mouthpiece is a swan's neck, elephants are like various brass instruments.*

Con delicatezza,
The Maestro, Souvenir Press.

A whole chapter of Hoffnung's Musical Chairs *is devoted to music and the animal world. The piano was Hoffnung's favourite source of similes: it is a billiards table, a fishing pond, a hippopotamus, a bull in a bullring, and many other things besides. Water is a prominent con-comitant of Hoffnung's musical humour—perhaps because he was a blower (of the ocarina as well as the tuba) himself, and fair wind always brings foul water with it. Hence, in the 1956 Hoffnung Festival, the water-bottles in Haydn's* Surprise Symphony, *and the unrealised project of a gargling chorus to be composed by Matyas Seiber.*

Many of these drawings examine the literal implications of a name: the serpent swallows its performer, the double bass is double and re-

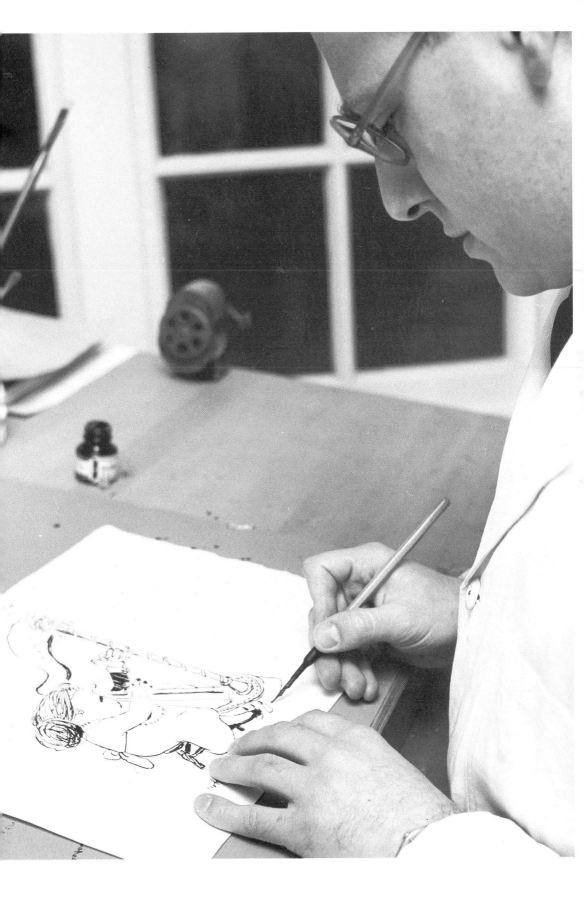

quires two players – which leads to the double violin, 'clef' means key, and so the musician unlocks his door with a treble clef. Brass instruments must surely include the brass bedstead, the ideal instrument on which to perform Eine Kleine Nachtmusik. The lady who knits at a concert forgets her pattern in her absorption, and knits a trumpet.

But for the most part Acoustics is about visual equivalents of audible sounds, as its title suggests. This seems to me the most remarkable and promising of all Hoffnung's musical joke sources, because the humour here is purely musical.

The most imaginative of all these drawings, tantalisingly far-reaching, are the pictures of Noises: the unbroken ridged pelmet for 'legato', the Klee-ish 'pizzicato', the Chagallesque 'arpeggio', and the contorted drum-roll. And in a new, extremely fetching style, the demure four-note chord and shrieking discord. The phantom double-bass and the matchstick oboe, the dull smudge of the bass drum, and the luxuriant bunch of flowers sprouting from the trumpet – in all these, Hoffnung's genius travelled far from the modest caricatures that were his first musical drawings. He was on the verge of pure musical draughtsmanship and a completely uncharted artistic territory. Hoffnung's Acoustics only hints at what was due to emerge from that ambitious imagination. 'The world,' wrote E. B. White, 'decorates its serious artists with laurel, and its wags with Brussels sprouts.' Hoffnung received his accolades of sprouts; but music meant so much to him that he would sooner or later have qualified for laurels as well.

Quite a different challenge confronted him in November 1952 when he was invited to speak at the Cambridge Union. The motion of the debate was 'This House resents growing up and regrets growing old'. Alistair Sampson who was president of the Union at the time, described the occasion of Gerard's visit:

Gerard came and gave one of the most superb comic oratoric performances that the Union can ever have heard. Devoid of cruelty and vulgarity, it was a superb example of pure humour. He was enchanting, fascinating and tumultuous. One moment he was offering snuff to his undergraduate audience, the next he was touching the microphone and leaping back as though electrocuted. His memories of a Turkish Bath were perhaps the most memorable of all.

During the ensuing years he made three further visits – once to debate the motion

'If music be the food of love, play on', when he played what he called his 'Stradivarius Tuba' for a full ten minutes, surely an unprecedented activity in a University debating chamber. The University newspaper, Varsity, *said of another visit, 'He was funnier than anyone has been at the Union before'.*

So it is that others may remember him as musician, conversationalist or cartoonist, but I think of him as a speaker. He had all the graces for which those who analyse good speaking look – sympathy, observation, style and masses of audibility. He felt very deeply about many aspects of social and political life, but always at the back of his mind was the desire to keep the world sane with laughter.

Alistair goes on to relate one of his favourite Hoffnung anecdotes: *The story concerns the* Tonight *programme at the time of the Suez Crisis. On an evening while the crisis was at its height Gerard was billed to discuss some innocuous and disassociated subject – probably a Hoffnung Music Festival. During the rehearsal he casually but seriously told one of the production staff that the moment he was in vision he intended to look straight into the cameras and say, 'Eden must go!' Not surprisingly this, coming a few minutes before Gerard was due to appear, caused the programme to develop a Crisis all of its own. There were consultations behind the scenes as to what should be done. It was decided that Gerard should be warned that if he showed any signs of carrying out his threat he would at once be faded out. In the final minutes before Gerard's part in the programme began, the Director was*

Gerard at the Cambridge Union in 1952. On the left of the President, Alastair Sampson, seated centre, is the actor A.E. Matthews. On his right are Gerard and Gilbert Harding.

to be seen making switching-off signs at Gerard from behind the glass-panelled control-room to remind him of what would be done if he did not behave, while Gerard in return was repeatedly mouthing the words, 'Eden must go!' When his time came all went well and the BBC heaved a sigh of relief—but to the end they never knew whether this was a gigantic leg-pull or whether he had indeed only just succeeded in re-straining himself from giving vent to his feelings.

The obvious success of his Union speech and the reception it received was an eye-opener to Gerard of his capabilities as an entertainer.

He returned to Cambridge a year or two later, this time to debate 'This House prefers Newnham to Girton because it is further away'. Gerard was very taken by the girls of Newnham who not only invited him to tea beforehand but also wrote a calypso in his honour, took him boating and generally made a fuss of him.

Commenting the following day, the local paper said:

Turkish baths: 'They were wrapped in long white sheets, like ghosts...'

... Then came Gerard Hoffnung. To describe the mixture of clowning and story-telling adequately is impossible. He went his way like an animated cartoon with a small touch of surrealism. He did not make the mistake of discussing the motion; the nearest he got to it was: 'I think that Girton is very far away indeed. Not as far as it should be and not as far as Newnham. ...'

Later, when Gerard was invited back, appropriately enough, to debate the motion 'If music be the food of love, play on' with a fellow speaker in the person of John Dankworth, a tuba and a clarinet were ceremoniously brought in by two attendants towards the end of the proceedings and the students were treated to some quite ravishing solos and duets.

The last union debate Gerard attended was his first at Oxford and the only one that was recorded. For a long time I used to hope that tapes of his Cambridge speeches would be discovered in some dark corner of the Cambridge Union, but as time went by it seemed a less and less likely possibility. Tape recorders were not so readily available then. In those speeches Gerard told the stories with which I had become so familiar over the years and which never failed to amuse me. It is very satisfying to see people shaking with laughter. There was his long saga of the hedgehog he discovered one night on the back porch which refused the bread and milk he put out for it and in the morning turned out to be a lavatory brush Marie had left out to air. There were the lengthy and hilarious ramifications of the account of his first visit to a Turkish bath. His repertoire was considerable.

Good fortune attended us all when the BBC decided to record the Oxford Union Debate on Thursday, 4 December 1958. 'Life begins at thirty-eight' was the motion for debate, though only at the very end, for a few serious moments, did Gerard touch on the subject. Instead he wooed his audience with nonsense after nonsense till, as one can hear on the recording of the proceedings, they became weak with laughter. He told, amongst others, the Story of the Bricklayer which soon became, and remains, one of the most popular pieces of Hoffnung lore. The story itself is as old as the hills. Christopher Logue once told me that he had traced it as far back as 1926. It concerns a bricklayer's experiences when, with the assistance of a pulley, he hoists some bricks to the top of a building and afterwards returns the remaining ones back down again. I have always imagined it to be some sort of Harold Lloyd sequence in a silent film, so visual is its appeal. This particular version Gerard found one day in the *Manchester Guardian*. It says little for my imagination and sense of humour that when he first showed it to me I didn't find it particularly amusing. He cut the piece out, folded it neatly into his wallet and carried it with him in his breast pocket. At the slightest opportunity he would draw it out decorously and declaim it to his friends and acquaintances. The fact that the more he told this story the more he enjoyed it, and the more often people heard it the more they enjoyed it too, must, I think, have something to do with the law of comic dynamics, the tantalising fun of waiting for the final denouement. The painstaking elaboration, the crazy chain of cause and effect, the Chaplinesque personality of the well-meaning, unfortunate little man and the sudden deflatory sentence at the end when, his saga over, he abruptly signs off – all this gave Gerard full scope for his love of heightened drama and his sense of timing. He so obviously relished every moment of it.

Benedict Hoffnung announces
his arrival on the fourth of April, 1955
and sends you his kindest regards.

In our home, work and play combined and life was good. In 1955 we eagerly anticipated the arrival of a 'lodger'. 'I'm sorry we cannot make any arrangements for next April because we are expecting a lodger to stay,' Gerard told puzzled listeners with great seriousness. The arrival of our son, Benedict, was one of the great joys of our life together, and the birth three years later of our daughter, Emily, completed our happiness. Filled with feelings of responsibility after the birth of our first-born, we negotiated with our landlord, who agreed to sell us his interest in the property. I did not realise at the time the blessing this would prove to be later on. The purchase was made on a mortgage endowment policy, which meant that on Gerard's death the children and I had the security of a home. It meant we could remain in our familiar surroundings.

My three-week stay in hospital prior to Benedict's birth gave Gerard an insight into a life that was unfamiliar to him. I think it

Arrival of Benedict.

Emily's birth announcement card. Drawing from *Hoffnung's Little Ones* Souvenir Press.

Emily Hoffnung

announces her

distinguished

arrival on

Friday 11th April 1958

and sends you

her compliments

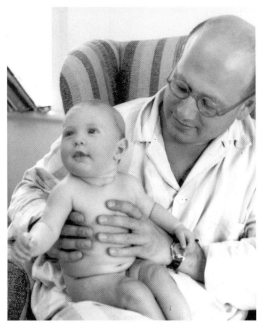

Gerard with Benedict (*left*) and Emily (*right*).

must have been the constant measuring of my blood-pressure that inspired him to his own version of this operation. I can still hear one of the Sisters saying to him firmly on an occasion when he was getting himself well and truly into an anxious state, 'You must not worry Mr Hoffnung – we've never lost a father yet.'

And there was the time when he took a rather severe matron's hand, placed it ceremoniously under his arm and with a conspiratorial nod to her said 'Come along matron my dear, you and I are going to take a look at my son.'

Lady with high blood pressure, *Hoffnung's Harlequinade.*

Cats and flowers, a previously
unpublished drawing.

Visit to an art gallery,
The Isle of Cats, Scolar Press.

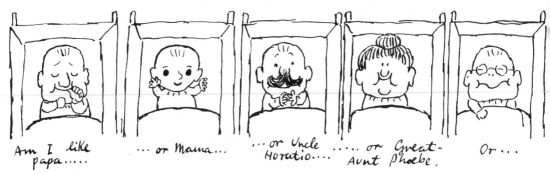

Am I like papa..... ... or Mama... ...or Uncle Horatio.... ..... or Great-Aunt Phoebe. Or...

Most aptly, Gerard at this time was illustrating a weekly article in the *Daily Express* written by Lady Elizabeth Pakenham and entitled 'Points for Parents'. These articles, along with some of the illustrations, were published in a book of the same title. Later still, in 1961, a collection of the drawings only was brought out in a book called *Hoffnung's Little Ones*.

... am ...

..I... ...like... ...some... ....body... ..else.

Or am I like me?

Two drawings from *Hoffnung's Little Ones*, Souvenir Press. One of the drawings from the collection combines Gerard's love of children and cats.

Gerard also enjoyed illustrating a book of poems by Percy Cudlipp entitled *Bouverie Ballads*. One of my favourite poems is

DO BISHOPS BROOD?

*Clergy and laymen protested against a portrait of the
Bishop of Chichester which gave a "brooding and pugnacious expression"
to his kindly face*

> In Chichester-cathedral town
>   Ensconced attractively
> Beneath the undulating down,
>   Adjacent to the sea —
> In Chichester, so staid and pleasant,
> Tempers are running high at present.
>
> Then what, you ask me, has occurred
>   To mar the cloistral peace,
> And why are furious mutterings heard
>   Throughout the diocese?
> The people's wrath o'erflows its vial
> Because they love their Bishop's dial.
>
> "We'd like", they said, "Right Reverend sir,
>   To have you done in oils."
> 'Tis finished now, and Chichester
>   Abhorrently recoils.
> Old ladies who have seen the painting
> Assure me they came near to fainting.
>
> Was this the face they knew so well,
>   The mild familiar phiz
> Of Dr. G. K. Allen Bell —
>   This brooding visage his?
> "He's made the Bishop look pugnacious!
> Impossible! Absurd! Good gracious!"
>
> And rural dean to canon cried
>   "Protest we surely must!"
> And curates with their vicars vied
>   In horror and disgust.
> The loyal laity's allergy
> Matched the repugnance of the clergy.

Oh wretched artist! It may be
　　You sought to paint a mood,
Convinced in all sincerity
　　That even bishops brood.
In Chichester such thoughts are alien
To every true episcopalian.

Gerard was an admiring and devoted father and, because he worked from home a good deal of the time, he was more closely involved with his children than he might otherwise have been. Some things he found difficult, if not impossible to tolerate, but most situations, with a little judicious planning and strategy, could be circumnavigated. He disliked untidiness and messiness in any form, especially where eating was concerned. It offended him and made him unhappy. 'I am put off my food. I cannot eat,' he would complain. (Some may have considered this not such a bad thing for his rotund figure.) From very early on, father and son developed an understanding of each other which sometimes surprised onlookers. One summer afternoon we were having tea with friends in the garden. Benedict was being fractious and after a little while Gerard had had enough. Our friends clearly remember his words. 'Listen my boy! There's a brace and bit in the garage and if you don't stop this nonsense I'm going to get it out and I'll bore holes all over and right through you. You'll leak out all over the place and a proper mess it will be,' threatened Gerard. 'You'll have nothing left inside you.' There was not a flicker of anything but intense interest on Benedict's face. As Gerard elaborated (there was also the further horror of a saw in the garage) so Benedict's eyes grew bigger and bigger as he

became totally engrossed in this grotesque story. His bad mood evaporated and both storyteller and listener became more and more fascinated by the possibilities of further dreadful perpetrations.

During the last four years of happy domestic life, Gerard's creativity and activity reached its height. His output was prolific and might give the impression that he spent his entire time bent over his drawing board. This was not so. Pressures there were and plenty of them, but we also led a very full and engaging life, visiting and entertaining friends, going to the theatre, opera and concerts, and sometimes taking a holiday.

My friend, Morag Morris, frequently visited us in those days. She once described in *O Rare Hoffnung* her impressions of our household. When I read her account I am immediately transported back to those happy days.

One might call at his home at mid-morning, as I used to, to see his wife, and Gerard would descend to the kitchen, vermilion pyjamas beneath his dressing-gown, in an aroma of cleanliness, bland and beaming – and suddenly ply one with serious questions, expecting a prompt and constructive reply. Or one might arrive at the back door to a ringing of telephone and door bells and children chanting, and Gerard above in frantic falsetto voice, adding to the chaos with schoolboy glee. Or he might burst from his study in a crisis of despair, exaggerated in self-mockery and love of drama. There was a robust and all-embracing rightness about his life.

Gerard was also a keen cinema-goer, his particular delight being the horror film. To my relief he discovered a kindred spirit in our friend George Engle, thereby liberating me from much suffering. Their happy hours spent together at the cinema would be followed by earnest discussion and debate on every tiny aspect. George recalls Gerard's love of the macabre:

The Hoffnung Music Festival, yes – but what about the Hoffnung Festival of Horror? This should have been a treat in store for us – a collection of hand-picked horror films shown in a full Hoffnung setting, with monsters prowling among the audience. It was this that Gerard hoped

for, when he brought his encyclopaedic knowledge of cinemato-graphic horrors to the arrangement of a series of horror films at the National Film Theatre. Alas, when it came to the point, many of the films which Gerard wanted shown were found to be completely unobtainable – where he had managed to see some of them himself is a mystery – and there was no money for monsters. Gerard was, I remember, very disappointed; but he produced for the outside of the programme a memorable drawing of a rakish vampire greedily suc-king at a glass of blood – through a straw.

Gerard's relish for the macabre was full-blooded and infectious. Just as, at meals, when the mood took him, he would play a few bars on the tuba between courses, so without warning he would turn away for a moment and reappear as one of his favourite monstrosities – a feroci-ously lopsided Quasimodo, maybe, or the nameless old man, one-eyed and wry-necked, who lurches down the back stairs of that terrible inn at the beginning of Carl Dreyer's Vampyr. *He loved to enact whole scenes from his favourite film,* The Old Dark House *– a really terrible film, he called it once, in a broadcast. He would be Morgan, the dumb manserv-ant (Karloff's part) opening the door; or the fanatical and alarming Miss Femm; or, best of all, the homicidal pyromaniac Saul, with his clipped and crafty talk ('I've made a study of flames. They're like knives') and his sudden mad cackle. At other times he would give you the sinister coachman in* Dead of Night, *croaking in gleeful tones his sepulchral 'Just room for one more inside, Sir', or the horrible Agatha Payne in Hugh Walpole's* The Old Ladies, *consumed with an insane craving to possess the harmless Miss Beringers' treasured piece of amber. There was no end to these impersonations, for Gerard had a wonderful gift of mimicry, and if he didn't quite understand some hor-rible piece of business in a film or book, he would as likely as not do it for you, and then, in a puzzled and slightly impatient way, demand to know what exactly it all meant.*

I remember exactly how Gerard transformed himself into Quasimodo. To create the effect took him no more than a few seconds. First he would pull his nose to one side and secure it with a piece of sellotape. Into his mouth would go a plate of false, projecting, front teeth – the sort available in joke shops – and down the back of his jacket he would stuff a cushion to create a hump. A peculiarity of Gerard's was that he could roll his right eye round in a complete circle while his left remained still. I am not sure how he managed this, but it was all part of the performance. With

his head drawn over on one side, shuffling and limping along and puffing and snuffling away, the effect was a combination of scariness (especially if he came really close and stared you straight in the eye) and ridiculous fun-making. One dark night he excelled himself by going outside and appearing at the sitting-room window – quite a surprise to our friends who were not aware of this game that Gerard played. Pressing his nose against the glass gave added effect. In a moment of rashness I locked him outside and as he rampaged around the house looking unsuccessfully for another place of entry, I had really to pluck up courage to let this monster in again! As with his cat imitation, one was aware that the whole thing was fantasy, yet despite the nonsense there was something persuasive and plausible about it all and therefore convincing.

Another friend of Gerard's, John Inglis Hall, wrote:

. . . being un-sinister, he put such tremendous energy into being sinister that he made it almost as menacing as the real thing. He could put down a clarinet in its case, or an ocarina in its little box, and run from it with such exquisite terror, blocking his ears, that it became instantly an infernal machine. He used also to announce his arrival for dinner by playing any musical instrument he happened to have with him, through the letter box, which he propped open with the evening paper. There was nothing farcical about these performances. If there was intention in them, it was only to give pleasure to everyone, including himself, and to banish solemn care. He added:

Even when he met you and said 'Good evening', there was something in the look he gave you, peering rather theatrically over the top of his glasses, that hinted at the imminence of some absurd catastrophe or phantasmagoric succession of strange events in which he would shortly take part, to the alarm of the orthodox. He represented a constant threat to everybody's normal behaviour. One was tempted to join in.

He did not need a large audience to enact these fanciful flights of his imagination. Occasionally when I awoke him in the morning (Gerard was a late riser) he would go through great lengths of absurdities. One I remember in particular was his burlesque of death at its most macabre. He would suddenly sit up in bed for a moment and then fling himself violently back on his pillows, his face contorted into whatever grotesque expression he could conjure up. Sometimes his eyes were shut, sometimes open and staring wildly. Once the right eye suddenly revolved in a circle, and that was the most sinister of the lot! But as always this caricature of a situation was excruciatingly funny, more especially if he happened to be wearing his nightcap at the time.

Facial expressions were a constant fascination. Leaving his draw-

NATIONAL FILM THEATRE

Programme

Price Sixpence

ing board and peering into the mirror above his mantelpiece, Gerard would become his own model, experimenting not only with the extremes of distortion and grimace but probing, too, the more subtle elements of surprise, curiosity, effrontery, dismay, until he was confronted by exactly the desired effect he wished to express in his drawing.

Other people's faces were a constant source of interest too. I remember the tolerance and amiability of our friend, Wilfred Stiff, at whose home we were dining on an evening when Gerard suddenly arrived at the notion that Wilfred's face had all the visual makings of a perfect clown. Excited by this arresting and unexpected prospect, the young son of the house quickly produced a box of water-colours. After this there could be no holding back. For half an hour Wilfred succumbed to Gerard's concentrated application of paint and then, after a time spent by those present in delighted admiration of the transformation, soap and water eradicated all trace.

None of these activities affected the steady flow of work from his drawing board. Early on in his career Gerard had been approached by the advertising world, and by 1946 he was producing a series of 'Kia-Ora' advertisements. Even piston rings, packaging and paint

Advertisement for pi ton rings from Lockwood and Carlis Ltd.

...and **our** rings

prevent escapes, too!

inspired his imagination in most curious ways. For Pegson Ltd no drawing was needed at all – merely a photograph of Gerard and his good friend Joseph Horovitz, composer of a work performed at a recent Hoffnung concert which used the road-rammer on the platform of the Royal Festival Hall to augment the orchestral percussion. In a similar vein, the management of Hoover chose to combine the advertising of their wares with a Hoffnung concert, while the clients of Pall Mall were greeted musically at Christmas time.

Advertisement for
Esso Chemicals.

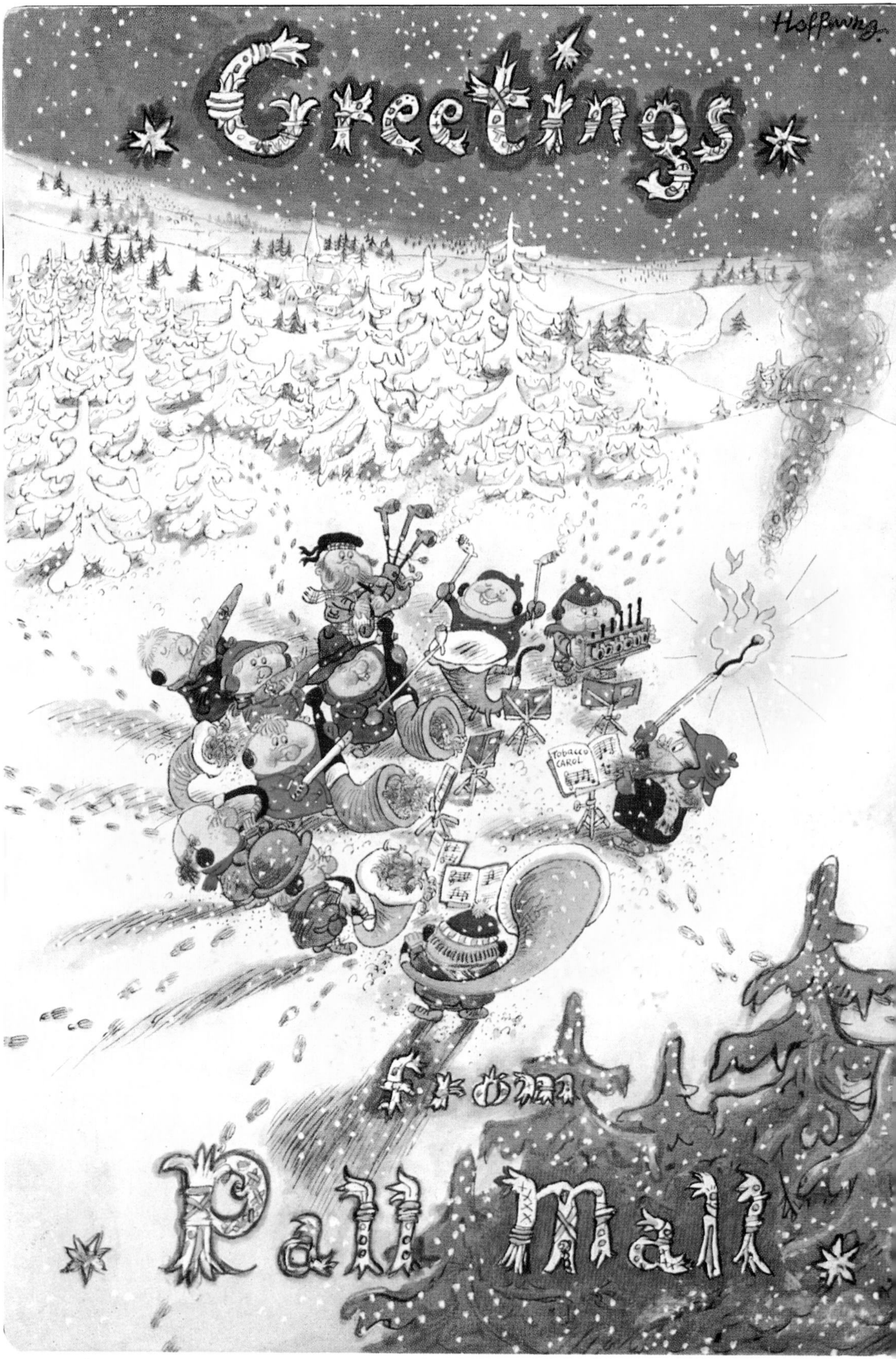

Hoffnung
Greetings
Tobacco Carol
from
Pall Mall

The Guinness publication, *Reigning Cats and Dogs*, suddenly displayed a whole lot of Hoffnung dogs. In view of the title, this was not unexpected, but as if to compensate, the booklet contains what I think is Gerard's most magnificent cat: Kipling's cat.

Stray Doggerel

THE SHIH TSU
At Shows, you sometimes see on view
This sweet Tibetan bitch,
But judges seldom have a clue
Which shih tsu's end is which.

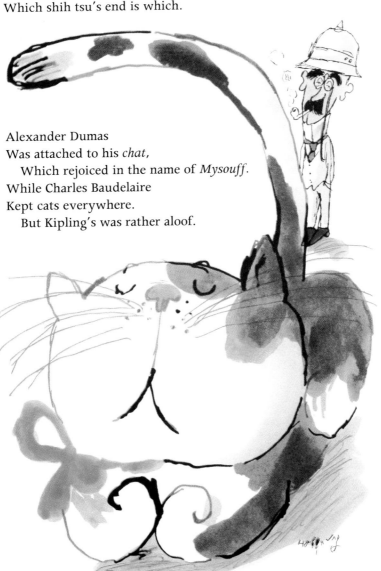

Alexander Dumas
Was attached to his *chat*,
   Which rejoiced in the name of *Mysouff*.
While Charles Baudelaire
Kept cats everywhere.
   But Kipling's was rather aloof.

Gerard's love and admiration for feline creatures did not diminish
with the years. I like the cat he drew for our Christmas card one year
and also the dear lady who carves a turkey for her guest of honour.
Some early Christmas cards that survive all contain cats. In one, the
little prisoner in his cell has no feline companion, though the present
left in his Christmas stocking should do much to cheer him up.

Merry Christmas

Starting the Turkey.

All good wishes from
Gerard

for Annette
from Uncle

A little Christmas card from Sir Gerard Hoffnung
Christmas
Greetings!!!
Bon.

A lovely
Turkey for
Annette

for Miss Bennett
from Mr Hoffnung

For Annette
Bennett from
uncle Hoffnung.

Merry
Christmas

Gerard's musical drawings and his prowess on the tuba brought him many new friends in the world of music. These absorbing and exciting contacts provoked his inventive mind. They also provided fresh subjects for caricature, though he was not always pleased with the results. Once, even after determined effort, John Dankworth's personality still eluded him. Frustrated, Gerard abandoned the attempt with disappointment and a feeling that he had in some way failed a good friend.

As he was finishing work on the third book of musical caricatures early in 1956, he reflected on why it should be that music was the only art form deprived of comedy. Humour had until then had relatively little outlet in musical performance, although musicians so often display a spontaneous sense of fun. Visually, humour in art had readily been accepted for centuries. Hogarth, Rowlandson, Daumier and, in our day, Steinberg were not merely funny men; their pictures had a place in leading art galleries.

From the early days of orchestral composition, composers had inserted jokes into their works (Mozart best of all practised this habit). Yet there was no great humorous composer. Gerard recalled the intimate evenings of musical humour popular in this country in the past. As long ago as 1946 the BBC's Third Programme broadcast delightful concerts of musical curiosities and humour devised by Humphrey Searle in collaboration with other composers – Alan Rawsthorne, Constant Lambert, and E. J. Moeran among them. 'Funny' concerts were a more recent phenomenon, and Gerard had taken part in one or two of them. He once played a bicycle pump in an April Fool's day event devised by Denby Richards in the Recital Room of the Royal Festival Hall. They were popular entertainments, usually noted for their informality, improvisation and, quite often, lack of organisation.

Gerard journeyed once or twice to Liverpool to play his tuba in a similar concert devised by Fritz Spiegl. Donald Swann recalled, when I spoke to him recently, that he also took part in one of the Liverpool concerts with Gerard – or, at least, very nearly – for the evening stretched to such inordinate lengths that the time limit was reached before he was able to perform his piece. Travelling back on the train to London the next day, he remembers Gerard saying that it seemed to him there was room for something that would really put the comedy of music on the map in a big way. He envisaged a fabulous Music Festival of symphonic caricature with a vast

The composer, Humphrey Searle, also a great lover of cats.

orchestra and soloists performing works specially commissioned from leading composers. Later, the idea was announced at a press conference and *The Times* reported on this with dignity: *If we take him aright, he wishes to purge our concert-going of its habitually imperceptive solemnity to indicate the humour in music we forget to notice. A breath of fresh air in the arts is a blessing.*

John Amis organised the first Hoffnung concert.

While the *Yorkshire Post* had this to say:
... By the time Mr Hoffnung came to the end of his announcements, his arms were shooting out in all directions as if he were already conducting from the rostrum. Suddenly he became serious, and his high-pitched voice fell half an octave. 'It is a serious attempt by my colleagues and myself to bring caricature into symphonic music.'

A favourite restaurant of Gerard's – Wheeler's in Soho – was the venue chosen for an auspicious occasion to which a number of people were invited to lunch one day. I had my misgivings – the restaurant was expensive and the list of guests long. They included Ernest Bean, the General Manager of the Royal Festival Hall, people from the BBC, EMI, the record company, Eric Thompson from the Arts Council, Dennis Dobson, Gerard's publisher, also John Amis, an old friend who was to organise the first concert and to contribute so excellently to the second one, and the impresario, Ian Hunter, all curious as to their host's intent. It was not until the coffee that Gerard produced his notes and started to explain his plan to his guests.

It was to be a concert to end all concerts. It would consist of entirely new music, not one note of which, at that time, had been written. It was to be, explained Gerard, a concert of such brilliance and artistic merit that it would create a sensation, a combination of superb clowning and good music with the cream of the music profession taking part. And it should take place at the Royal Festival Hall. Possible instrumentation must have been discussed at this meeting because strange rumours soon began to circulate of road-rammers, hot-water bottles and vacuum cleaners filling unlikely roles. Before the gathering dispersed, Mr Bean had decided that the Royal Festival Hall, then under the auspices of the London County Council, should sponsor the concert and make available a suitable evening later in the year for the occasion. It was April then and the concert was scheduled for November. In the intervening months, ideas sprang

Ernest Bean, the General Manager of the Royal Festival Hall.

up all over the place, works were commissioned, performers' part-
icipation agreed, posters and programmes designed, and collaborators cajoled in a frenzy of activity I had not experienced before.
Gerard had a knack for triggering off the creative abilities of conductors, composers, artists, soloists and musicians. It was a gift that
stood him in good stead, for without the concerted effort of this host
of fundamentally serious musicians, his visions could not have
materialised. He countered any misgivings, secured their commitment, and enthused and encouraged all involved. They in turn responded with remarkable goodwill and tolerance to the unusual and
sometimes outrageous demands made upon them.

At home we took delivery of an enormous contra-bass serpent, an
aged, rare and valuable instrument kindly loaned by the Tolson
Memorial Museum in Huddersfield. It arrived earlier than expected
and spent the month prior to the concert lying the length of our
sitting-room sofa, an interesting if awkward guest. The alphorn,
(photograph on p.134) stretched down the stairway and across the
hall. Fortunately for us, the giant bass drum, over eight feet in
diameter, was delivered direct to the Royal Festival Hall, as was the
monster tuba, made at the turn of the century for Sousa. It stood
over six feet tall and I think I need hardly mention who played this
instrument on the night of the concert. One newspaper remarked
afterwards: 'Mr Hoffnung played a tuba the size of a blast furnace.
Although born in 1925 one cannot suppress the conviction that in
fact he sprang fully grown from the bell of this large instrument.'

Ernest Bean, to whom reference has already been made, wrote
about these lively times:

In the course of a year hundreds of famous artists visit the Royal Fes-
tival Hall. But there has never been anyone like Gerard Hoffnung. He
didn't visit *the Festival Hall; he* invaded *it. He*
invaded it with gales of laughter and with
the gusto of a great comic personality. I
learned to know when Gerard was in
the vicinity of the South Bank from the
glint of madness and the joyous air of
irresponsibility in the eyes of attend-
ants, finance officers, cleaners, electri-
cians and car-park attendants whose
paths he had happened to cross. When
he was around, the Festival Hall took on
the atmosphere of a Rene Clair film set!

I would not say that he was an easy
man to work with when he was mounted on

Franz Reizenstein, the
composer of *Concerto
Popolare*.

one of his wild hobby-horses! Between the moment that a Hoffnung fantasy was conceived and the night of the concert none of his confederates could call his life his own. They were all liable to be telephoned in the dead of night to be told of the latest outrageous quirk which had alighted athwart the nose of our Mercutio as he lay asleep.

I remember one such occasion vividly. One morning there was a knock at my door. After a portentous pause the door opened and inch by inch, foot by foot, there advanced into my room, like the floating objects which enlivened spiritualist seances, a long metal tube with a horn like an elephant's proboscis. When it had filled the whole length of my office there appeared at the business end, like a conception from one of his own cartoons (I sometimes suspected that Gerard's cartoons were in actual fact self-portraits seen through a distorted mirror) the round, smiling, cherubic face of Gerard Hoffnung.

'What do you think of this?' he asked. 'Let me play it to you . . . But it's no use here . . . there isn't room . . . I'll tell you what! You go into the street: I'll put the end through the window: and you can hold an audition from there!'

I endeavoured to point out that the extensive building operations then taking place on the South Bank, with giant electric pile-drivers making the day hideous, would prevent me hearing a note of the music. But he gave me that knowing, conspiratorial smile, the like of which I have never seen on any other human face, and gently urged me to do as I was told. As usual, I did. He put the mouthpiece to his lips. A look of unalloyed bliss suffused his features. And he began to play the Prelude to Lohengrin!

I need not have worried about my ability to hear the performance. I

The arrival of the alphorn.

could have heard it from Greenwich. It filled the whole of the South Bank. The electric drills stopped. Passing motorists on the Victoria Embankment swerved dangerously. Day-dreaming pedestrians started in wild surmise. And I, in fear of being apprehended from committing a public nuisance, sought sanctuary in my office.

Although the emphasis of humour in the concerts was manifest in the music itself, Gerard allowed his visual sense of fun full scope. A sedan chair, carried by four elegant bewigged pages in rococo uniform, was used to transport some of the more privileged participants

Gerard playing the monster tuba at the Royal Festival Hall in Dr Gordon Jacob's *Variations on a theme of Annie Laurie.*

onto the platform. Thirty-eight fanfare trumpeters from the Royal Military School of Music, in full regalia, brought visual as well as aural colour to the proceedings. One of the additional surprises arranged by Donald Swann in the andante from the *Surprise Symphony* by Haydn was a dancer who wafted daintily across the platform. A large bouquet, indeed almost a hamper, of vegetables was presented to the pianist Yvonne Arnaud, beloved actress, comedienne and musician, after her performance of the *Concerto Popolare*.

The public, by this time, anticipating that something rare, if not unique, was about to descend upon London, played their part, and when the Festival Hall Box Office opened, all tickets were sold out in under two hours, beating even the record of Liberace. The BBC announced that they would broadcast the first half of the concert on television, and amidst frenzied activity events got further under way. Rehearsals were scheduled, and nervous tension increased as the day approached when the newly-commissioned music would be heard for the first time.

Yvonne Arnaud receiving her bouquet of vegetables.

Sam Wanamaker, our producer, remembers:

The first full rehearsal with Lawrence Leonard's Morley College Orchestra was approached with a kind of controlled horror over the hoax we were about to perpetrate on an unsuspecting public. There was no turning back. Here we were, by now hundreds of people involved, driven by Gerard's enthusiasm, and yet I had a strong premonition that it would all end in a terrifying shambles of amateur hijinks. The members of the orchestra sheepishly awaiting the start sceptically turned over the newly copied parts of Malcolm Arnold's overture which he was to conduct himself. Gerard took his place beside his tuba smiling broadly. It may have been only my own anxiety which made me think his grin was too wide this evening. At last Malcolm mounted the podium to conduct his Grand, Grand Overture *for three vacuum cleaners, a floor polisher, rifles and orchestra. He took up the baton and with a short 'Let's have a bash' raised the stick and gave the down beat. The impact of sound fairly lifted us all out of our seats. From time to time bursts of laughter from the non-blowing members of the orchestra greeted each audacious musical joke, nearly halting the wild flow as Malcolm flayed the air relentlessly. At the end of the piece, with Malcolm supplying the noises of vacuum cleaners and rifles in the appropriate places, the orchestra dissolved into a convulsion of helpless laughter. I knew then that the Hoffnung Festival Concert was well on the way to being a unique and wonderful experience – whatever happened.*

A lot of us were not too sure, even after the dress rehearsal on the morning of the concert, that this would be so! It was the only rehearsal to be held in the Royal Festival Hall. In the allotted three hours, attempts were made to bring some order to the vast forces that were now congregated in the hall. Confusion and a feeling of quiet hysteria ran rife.

We need not have worried. That night the vast hall exploded with mirth and the packed audience delighted in the evening of anarchic caricature. On arrival, there was no mistaking the festive atmosphere and the air of lively expectancy as a small military band in the foyer gaily piped a welcome to all comers. The audience, by now seated in the auditorium, sensed some measure of things to come as Ernest Bean made his brief announcement from the platform: 'Ladies and Gentlemen: owing to circumstances beyond the control of the London County Council and the management of this hall,' – the audience drew an anxious breath – 'tonight's concert will take place exactly as advertised'.

He was closely followed by Sir Thomas Beecham in person, or so it seemed, who gravely perambulated across the platform to place a score on the rostrum – a brilliant, bewigged and bewhiskered impersonation volunteered by one Ralph Nicholson. A critic pointed out a flaw in his performance – Sir Thomas's habit of always bowing to the orchestra before acknowledging the audience.

Published in the *Daily Mail*, 1956.

A pronounced drumroll indicated that all should rise for the National Anthem – but that too was a leg-pull. Immediately the audience was dazzled by an army of fanfare trumpeters playing an irrepressible little fanfare by Francis Baines.

Malcolm Arnold, in the company of three solo vacuum cleaners and a floor polisher, made his appearance. A sudden interruption at the rear of the hall turned all heads in the opposite direction and revealed Yfrah Neaman as an improbable and most impressive virtuoso lunatic busker. He ran through the auditorium, hotly pursued by two attendants, wearing shorts, a baggy raincoat and hat, giving a bravura performance of *The Irish Washerwoman*.

Eventually, the audience settled down to more serious (*sic*) entertainment as the *Grand, Grand Overture*, dedicated to President Hoover, got under way. With its rich sweeping melodies and the series of percussive climaxes in the endless, endless coda it did finally come to an end. As John Amis remarked in his programme note: 'If

VARNEY'S VIEW

" And furthermore, madam, this is the only model that beats as it sweeps as it cleans in C sharp minor."

the nature of the coda seems cursory it must be remembered that
Arnold always stops when he has nothing more to say.'

Donald Swann, aware that Haydn had written a drumroll into the
Surprise Symphony to wake up his somnolent audience, also knew
that despite this disturbance they very quickly went back to sleep
again. With this in mind he added a multitude of additional surprises
to the andante in order to keep the audience awake and alert
throughout. The performance culminated in a septet of stone hot-
water-bottle players gently blowing their way through the final
theme.

Dennis Brain, brilliant soloist, abandoned his horn for the hose-
pipe in a special arrangement by Norman Del Mar of Leopold
Mozart's *Concerto for Alphorn and Strings*. *The Times* next day said
'Mr Dennis Brain played a concerto on a coil of rubber hose-pipe
which emitted a faint but musical sound like a distant bugle call.'
Such was the enthusiasm of the players and the limitations of the
budget that many willingly performed for the love of it. Dennis,
after the performance, returned his cheque with a note.
*Thank you so much for your letters and cheque, which I am returning as
I think we arranged in the end that I should receive only expenses.*

Dennis Brain playing
Leopold Mozart's
*Concerto for Hosepipe
and Strings* conducted
by Norman del Mar.

These expenses, incidentally, amount to about half a dozen connec-tions, to join together the various experimental pieces of hosepipe now lying somewhat festooned about the garden!, and are more than balan-ced by being allowed to play the first instrument in the Royal Festival Hall that I have not had to practise – the organ in the Grand Overture. *My wife and I enjoyed the concert immensely, and look forward to the next.!*

John Betjeman wrote a poem entitled 'The Lift' expressly to show off the extraordinary range of Jenny Johnson's voice. This young lady could plumb the depths of a bass singer and soar above that of a normal soprano in a way that had to be heard to be believed. Donald Swann wrote and played the piano accompaniment.

THE LIFT

In uniform behold men stand
The lovely lift at my command
   I press the button. Pop.
And down I go below the town.
The walls rise up as I go down
   And in the basement stop.

For weeks I've worked a morning shift
On this old Waygood Otis lift
   And goodness, don't I love
To press the knob that shuts the gate
When customers are shouting 'Wait!'
   And soar to floors above.

I see them from my iron cage
Their faces looking up in rage
   And then I call 'First floor!
Perfume and ladies underwear!
No sir – Up only. Use the stair'
   And up again we soar.

The second floor for kiddie goods
And kiddie-pantz and pixie-hoods
   And third floor Restaurant
And here the people always try
To find one going down, so I
   Am not the lift they want.

On the roof-garden floor alone
I wait for ages on my own
 High, high above the crowds
O let them rage and let them ring
For I am out of everything
 Alone among the clouds.

Gerard, busily engaged throughout the evening as orchestral tuba player, was also soloist on several occasions. After his dissertation on the tuba ('Ladies and Gentlemen, I have been asked by the London County Council to make an announcement about this tuba. This is a Stradivarius tuba . . .') he was joined by three fellow tuba players who together gave a rendering of 'a nice delicate bit of Chopin'. He partnered Yvonne Arnaud in declaiming Sir Walter Scott's ballad *Lochinvar* (set by Humphrey Searle for eight percussion players) and he played on the monster tuba in Gordon Jacob's *Variations on a theme of Annie Laurie*, scored, in addition, for the contra-bass serpent (the only one in captivity, explained Gerard), and for serpent, two contra-bassoons, hecklephone, two contra-bass clarinets, two piccolos, harmonium and hurdy-gurdy – an odd collection of instruments for eye and ear.

Also performing were the Liverpool Chamber Music Singers under the lively conducting of Fritz Spiegl. They declaimed Ernst Toch's *Geographical Fugue*, and articulated place-names – Honolulu, Titicaca, Mississippi – with verve and precision. The highlight of the performance came when the conductor returned to the platform for an encore, to conduct the choir at breakneck speed as they frantically mimed their words to a speeded-up tape played off stage.

The composer, Dr Gordon Jacob, and Gerard seated on either side of the contra-serpent and surrounded by members of the Galpin Society.

Gerard and Yvonne
Arnaud declaiming
Lochinvar.

Orchestral Switch by Frank Butterworth was a sophisticated pot-pourri of forty-eight well-known themes so cleverly fused that some less musical members of the audience could be excused for believing it to be one continuous composition. No one has yet won the prize offered at each performance for the complete list of works.

Gerard's idea for a parody of the hostility that often exists between conductor and soloist on the concert platform was received with glee by Franz Reizenstein, composer of quiet genius. The orchestra was to start with the opening bars of Tchaikovsky's Piano Concerto No 1, only to be interrupted by the pianist determinedly making her entrance with Grieg's Piano Concerto. There were ideas for ensuing battles until the final denouement when both would vie for the final chord. Rarely has musical conflict been expressed with such openness on the concert platform. Franz produced a work, brilliant and ridiculous, that continues to delight Hoffnung concert audiences throughout the world. The photograph shows Franz, Gerard, Norman Del Mar, Yvonne Arnaud and Sam Wanamaker, all clearly bursting with ideas as *Concerto Popolare* took shape.

Although Gerard decided to bring

the concert to a close on a more serious note (Respighi's *Feste Romane*), this was absolutely in keeping with the spirit of the occasion. One critic wrote 'the final carnival left one feeling that Berlioz and Quo Vadis were milk and water beside this Roman Festival'. With an orchestra of one hundred players and accompanied by the thirty-six royal trumpeters it fairly lifted the roof off the Royal Festival Hall. Observant members of the audience could discern Malcolm Arnold among the trumpets and Norman Del Mar among the horns. Yvonne Arnaud played the piano, Hugo D'Alton the mandoline, and Dennis Brain was at the organ. Gerard was behind his tuba.

The response of the audience left no room for doubt about the success of the concert. It was a massive jamboree. EMI hurriedly issued the recording of the evening's event in time for Christmas.

Gerard approached the challenge of a second concert with caution. It was a challenge to meet and exceed the standard set by the first one. As usual he was up to his eyes in a number of other projects. We spent such a happy weekend at Glyndebourne, attending rehearsals or wandering through the grounds while Gerard explored ideas for a series of drawings for forthcoming Glyndebourne Opera programmes. From a box in the Royal Albert Hall we excitedly surveyed the spectacle of his designs for the Chelsea Arts Ball transformed into gigantic floating models. Sir Malcolm swung gently from the dome, baton poised. In a vast kettle-drum suspended in mid-air a surprised family of Hoffnung cats peered out at the scene below. Stretched across the width of the concert platform was an elongated and colourful concertina held at each end by two model players.

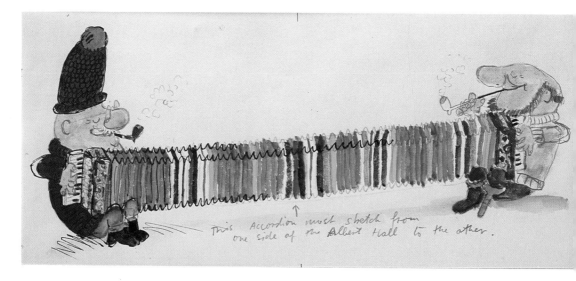

This Accordion must stretch from one side of the Albert Hall to the other.

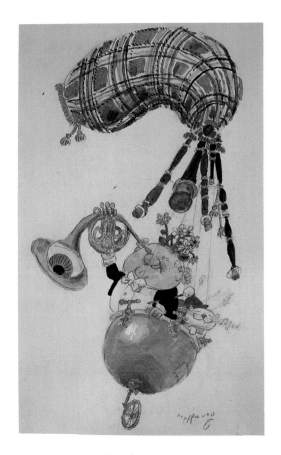

Designs for models for
the Chelsea Arts Ball
(*left and top*) and
(*below*) a drawing for
the Glyndebourne
Programme, *Hoffnung
in Harmony*, Souvenir
Press.

We went off on a skiing holiday. Gerard was surprisingly agile on the slopes. We journeyed for the day to nearby St. Moritz, drank hot chocolate at Hanselmann's cafe (of cherished childhood memory) and went to collect a trunk left by his mother at the Kulm Hotel in 1939. I remember little about the contents except the magnificent collapsible opera-hat that must have belonged to his father. But alas, there were no personal belongings of Gerard's that might have made an interesting and nostalgic discovery. In St. Moritz, he greatly coveted a pipe displayed in a window but discarded all thought of such an extravagant purchase. With some difficulty I swiftly and secretly amassed sufficient francs, then slipped away to buy it – a great surprise for his birthday later in the month.

All the time ideas for a new concert were flowing and more and more people were being drawn into the net. This time Gerard chose an outing to the zoo as a fitting occasion to announce his intentions to his fellow conspirators (so that the animals could be referred to for inspiration and advice, he explained). There was another reason for this gathering, as it also celebrated the award of an Oscar to Malcolm Arnold for the music he had written for the film *Bridge on the River Kwai*. Accordingly, Gerard chose to address the composer as Malcolm Oscar Arnold on his invitation.

After a noisy visit to the parrot house, the gathering watched the hippos being fed before moving on to the Fellows' dining room for lunch. Soon after, they learned of Gerard's high hopes for a Hoffnung Interplanetary Music Festival. Later, at a press conference, an Australian journalist asked 'But why Interplanetary?' Gerard, frowning, replied 'I am glad you asked me that because I don't know. It is, I think, symbolic of the immense proportions of this year's entertainment.'

The scale of the Hoffnung Interplanetary Music Festival was indeed vast. Taking part again were the 130-strong Festival Orchestra, alias Morley College Orchestra, the Royal Trumpeters from Kneller Hall, and in addition, a large operatic cast and chorus with soloists of international reputation. Once more the Royal Festival Hall was a record sell-out. Norman Del Mar was musical director. Colin Graham, acclaimed for his recent production of Britten's *Noyes's Fludde* and Stravinsky's *Soldier's Tale,* was our producer.

This time, unusual musical instruments were not a special feature, though a few out-of-the-way musical effects were planned. Some of these, alas, presented problems that were insoluble. It was *not* possible to have the Valkyries ride in on motor scooters because the London County Council forbad the use of petrol engines in theatres. ('Can't we tell them they run on cocoa?' pleaded Gerard.) The road-

Pauline del Mar on the road-rammer.

rammer, so admirably and convincingly introduced into the orchestra as a percussive instrument and bravely operated during the first concert by Pauline Del Mar, was forbidden a second hearing in view of the likely danger of the whole concert platform of the Royal Festival Hall collapsing onto the floor below. Even Gerard agreed that this would be carrying things a little too far, though I did discern a faraway look in his eye. Nor would the structure of the auditorium allow the leader of the orchestra to reach his place on the platform by tightrope.

But a ping-pong table, chosen for its particular resonance and interesting rhythm, was sited in the orchestra for the first time, as was the hiss of an Espresso coffee machine. This appliance fascinated him, said Gerard, not only for the strange sweet sound of the sea it produced but also because it always made him think of coffee.

It seemed that every national newspaper was eager to help us in our search for a small boy to play a watering can, none more solemnly than *The Times*. Eighteen came along to the Royal Festival Hall to be auditioned by Gerard in a blaze of television lights and radio mikes. Two were lucky.

Seven composers were commissioned by Gerard to write works for

Watering can auditions.

the forthcoming concert. The *Strad* magazine later made the following comment: 'It would be easy to turn a superior nose up at this concert, even though its success has been so tremendous that it is to be repeated in the New Year, but it is no mean achievement to have been able to induce so many people to listen to a programme by native contemporary composers, the name of any one of whom would normally be sufficient to empty the hall.' Francis Baines, Joseph Horovitz, Francis Chagrin, Matyas Seiber, Peter Racine Fricker, Franz Reizenstein and Malcolm Arnold all responded to the need for something in a lighter vein. And each and every one of them did so with obvious enthusiasm, none more brilliantly than Joseph Horovitz. In *Metamorphosis on a Bedtime Theme*, (played 'allegro commerciale in modo televisione') and using the slogan of a well-known milk beverage 'Sleep Sweeter Bournvita' he envisaged contributions the great composers might have made to the art of jingle writing for television. Scored for soprano, bass-baritone and harp, it was a brilliant pastiche. Alistair Sampson wrote the libretto, and April Cantelo and Ian Wallace performed it beautifully.

Gerard, always anxious to encourage music-making of all kinds in

Hoffnung Interplanetary Music Festival Poster, *Hoffnung in Harmony*, Souvenir Press.

HAROLD HOLT UNLIMITED IN ASSOCIATION WITH
THE LONDON COUNTY COUNCIL
PRESENTS:

The Hoffnung

INTERPLANETARY
MUSIC FESTIVAL
1958

ROYAL FESTIVAL HALL

General Manager: T.E. ⊕ C.B.E.

FRIDAY 21st AND repeated
SATURDAY 22nd NOVEMBER
at 8. p.m.

HOFFNUNG SYMPHONY ORCHESTRA
CONDUCTOR: LAWRENCE LEONARD.

HOFFNUNG FESTIVAL OPERA COMPANY
AND CHORUS

THE BAND AND TRUMPETERS OF THE ROYAL MILITARY
SCHOOL OF MUSIK (Kneller Hall) by permission of the Commandant
Lieut. Col. David McBain. O.B.E.

THE DOLMETSCH ENSEMBLE.

THE MAESTRO (only appearance in this country)
MALCOLM ARNOLD
AARON COPLAND
CARL DOLMETSCH
NORMAN DEL MAR
AND A SURPRISE CAST OF HUNDREDS!
PRODUCER: COLIN GRAHAM.

*An extravagant Gala Evening of Symphonic Caricature in glorious
Hoffnungscope, with a repeat performance. Eleven World premières
including THE UNITED NATIONS by Malcolm Arnold,
LET'S FAKE AN OPERA, an opera to end all operas by Franz Reizenstein,
and the first ever CONCERTO FOR CONDUCTOR AND ORCHESTRA by Francis Chagrin.
130 strong Symphony Orchestra loaded with Hoffnung
surprises, together with many of the world's most distinguished
composers and soloists. — Massed Bands and THE LOT !!!!!!*

TICKETS ON SALE OCTOBER 21st

15/-   12/6   10/6   7/6   5/-

From: ROYAL FESTIVAL HALL BOX OFFICE (WAT 3191), CHAPPELL'S, 50 NEW BOND STREET (MAY 7600),
USUAL Ticket Agents, and IBBS & TILLETT LTD., 124 WIGMORE STREET LONDON W.1. (WEL 8418)

DRAWINGS REPRODUCED FROM
THE HOFFNUNG CARTOON BOOKS
BY PERMISSION OF DOBSON~PUTNAM

the home, recognised one of his daintier visions in *Sugar Plums* realised by Elizabeth Poston. Here the celebrated Dolmetsch Ensemble,
together with Felix Aprahamian on miniature percussion and Elizabeth Poston herself on a portative organ, frolicked with some of the
great moments of the Tchaikovsky symphonies, thereby establishing
once and for all their place in the domestic scene. The battery, scaled
down accordingly to the size of a child's toy, was played by a team
of pop-gunners.

Ian Wallace and April
Cantelo.

Lionel Salter, Peter
Hemmings, Eric
Thompson and Robert
Ponsonby rehearse
with pop-guns.

Although Gerard had no experience of conducting, this was but a minor obstacle in his determination to succeed in an extravaganza planned for this new concert. Having commissioned a work from Francis Chagrin entitled *Concerto for Conductor and Orchestra* he spent a couple of days closeted with the leader of the Morley College Orchestra. Together they studied the score of this modern, and by no means easy, piece of music until Gerard decided he had mastered its intricacies. Some of his friends were understandably worried at the pitfalls they could envisage. Tentative plans were made to have a conductor to do the serious work, leaving Gerard free to clown. Gerard resisted with a quiet confidence. Of his performance on the night Thomas Heinitz wrote for *The Saturday Review*: 'Gerard Hoffnung displayed a hitherto unexpected facet of (his) many-sided talent. From the moment he bounded on to the rostrum to give his baton a rapier point with the aid of a pencil-sharpener until his final dash to the rear of the orchestra to shake hands with the tuba player, it was an exhibition worthy of Danny Kaye – culminating in a fearsome duel, all the way up the auditorium with a jealous solo pianist.' (none other than John Amis). That Gerard made it successfully to the end of fifteen minutes of modern symphonic music is even more remarkable when one looks at his 'score' (below)!

Gerard and John Amis duelling in the *Concerto for Conductor and Orchestra*.

Concerto for Conductor

1. Sharpening pencil, then : 5 beats

2. Rapping :

3. Upbeat : moderate $\frac{4}{4}$ (4 bars)

4. Harp Cadenza   Beat 1 2 3 4 at top of Harp gliss. then proceed.

5. March   Upbeat than steady $\frac{4}{4}$
   to Diminuendo ($\frac{4}{4}$ pauses, 1 silent)

6. Little bit of mucking about in moderate $\frac{4}{4}$

Nobody but Dame Edith Evans could have done justice to William McGonagall, Scottish poet and tragedian, included in the *Guinness Book of Records* as the worst poet in the English language. Dame Edith declaimed *The Famous Tay Whale* set to music and conducted by Matyas Seiber. Here the Espresso coffee machine came into its own visually as well as aurally with its jets of steam. I also took part, playing a splendid brass foghorn we had found the previous summer in an antique shop in Bognor Regis – thereby becoming, in a sense, a brass player after all.

With so many talented collaborators the concert went from strength to strength. Vicky, distinguished cartoonist for the *New Statesman*, recorded our activities. It was most unlikely that John Amis and Gerard would not put to good account their frequent telephone calls when they talked on endlessly to each other with pronounced and guttural German accents. In the end Gerard set John to write the script of a discussion between two German musicologists, Herr Dr. Domgraf Fassbender and Herr Professor von der Vogelweide who explain with Teutonic pomposity the deeper significance of a work by Bruno Heinz Ja-Ja, recently orchestrated from the electronic graph by Humphrey Searle. It was entitled *Punkt Contrapunkt*.

I remember the guffaws of laughter coming from Gerard's study as he and John rehearsed the script. Parts of it have already become classics and have been quoted to me by musicians throughout the

'Don't you think this joke has gone a bit too far?'.

world. One of the highlights was the awed and serious attention given by the two professors to the three bars of silence in Ja-Ja's work. 'The first is in $\frac{7}{8}$. The third also is in $\frac{7}{8}$. But the second bar of silence is in $\frac{3}{4}$ which gives the whole work a quasi-Viennese flavour.' Norman Del Mar conducted this section meticulously during the performance as the orchestra remained mute.

The final item in the first half of the concert was Malcolm Arnold's mammoth parody of national and international contrariety, a strange combination of trenchant satire and irrepressible burlesque entitled *United Nations*. At one point in this orchestral work no less than six royal military bands made their entrance into the concert hall. Each played its own national air or anthem and the bandsmen marched and counter-marched up and down the aisles while the 100-piece orchestra continued to play full force. Despite the cacophony, the work ended with a message of hope as the orchestral forces gradually subsided leaving a string quartet quietly playing the final notes of the noble opening theme.

One work alone, conducted by Norman Del Mar, filled the second half of the concert. A glittering array of singers from Sadlers Wells and Covent Garden took part in *Let's Fake an Opera*, a veritable operatic mayhem subtitled *Tales of Hoffnung*. Dozens of familiar operas (over forty of them) were ridiculously juxtaposed with delicious incongruity by William Mann into a libretto. Franz Reizenstein could not believe his eyes as he delightedly applied his talent and craftsmanship to the nonsense.

The complexities of the plot are immediately obvious when in the opening scene Beckmesser is found wooing a sexy Azucena outside a

cigarette factory in old Nuremberg. Salome cavorts in a dance of the
seven veils for Othello, revealing herself to be Fidelio and drawing
her pistols on him. Brünnhilde enters on her tricycle desperately
searching for a husband and disappointedly discovering Fidelio's
inadequacy to fulfil the role. She is further annoyed when Mélisande
appears at a window combing several yards of flaxen hair. But the
opera ends happily, for it is Radames who finally wins the prize song
(and Brünnhilde into the bargain) whereupon the happy couple make
a grand, triumphal exit followed by the cast. Except for the night-
watchman, that is, who with an eye for the main chance wearily
discovers the brass bedstead (a requisite rushed on to the platform at
one point for an exhausted coloratura) slumps on to it and with a
final 'cuckoo' on his horn, flops back on the pillows to sleep. Black
out.

So successful was this concert that two repeat performances followed a month or two later. Sol Hurok, the American impresario,
approached us from the other side of the Atlantic and we began
negotiations to put on a concert at the Berlin Festival in 1960.

Amidst such activity, Gerard worked on the sixth and last of his
little music books, *Hoffnung's Acoustics*, and on a book of non-
musical drawings entitled *Ho Ho Hoffnung* which were published by
Putnams. Trevor Poyser of Putnams worked closely with Gerard on
the actual production of these little books and describes his impressions of those times:

*Anyone who had the remarkable experience of working with Gerard
Hoffnung quickly discovered that for all his drollery and clowning he
was, if not a 'serious' artist, serious about his art. His sense of fun was
never long kept under, but the exacting care for the quality of reproduction and 'mise en page' of his work seemed almost in contra-
diction to the deceptive ease with which his pen drew the
fantasies. He would scrutinise the proofs of his drawings
with great thoroughness, consulting the originals and
demanding correction of the smallest imperfection. Like
most artists, and rightly, he would forget the publisher's
necessarily commercial point of view and that second
thoughts about the size of a drawing or the arrangement
of a page were costly. He found a disarming answer on
this point and would ask what was the most he might spend
on changes, a question which even a generous publisher
finds hard to answer precisely.*

*If, at times, one was exasperated by his insistence on
fidelity to the original drawing beyond the compass of the
reproduction process used, it was an instructive lesson in*

1926

what could be done by demanding perfection. But one was not allowed the relief of exasperation for long; having seen that the impossible was as nearly achieved as could be, he would revert to his hilarious normal self and the mood would evaporate in laughter, all forgotten. I recall only one occasion when he was unnaturally subdued when, during a visit to the printer, he watched the finished sheets of his book pouring from the press amidst the clatter and movement of machinery. Apart from the noise, which alarmed him, I believe it saddened him to find his creations at last beyond his care, and he watched disconsolately the mounting pile of printed sheets.

His visits to 42 Great Russell Street could disrupt the entire building, beginning with the switchboard and the despatch department and progressing boisterously upwards, department by department, to the third floor. He would take advantage of the moment to check on sales and stocks of his books and the size and date of the next reprint, and I remember his amazed delight on one occasion when he witnessed a collector's call from one of the larger wholesalers for an urgent and impressive quantity of his books.

His entrance into an office was seldom soberly done; an excessively discreet tapping on the door or a panel-shaking thump followed by eerie laughter was normal, as were the outrageous endearments with which he greeted secretaries and typists. He would explode into a room, beaming or scowling ferociously and, as likely as not, at once dash out again having forgotten to impart some gem of advice to the chairman or sales manager. His humour was never vindictive or coarse, and there was difficulty on one occasion in persuading him not to withdraw an ingenious but inoffensive cartoon which fashioned a W C from a tuba. A voice on the telephone asking for the Home Secretary or Fred O'Reilly was unlikely to be any but Gerard Hoffnung's, but once in a while he would phone to ask that, on his behalf, a few pounds be left in an envelope at reception against the visit of a newly released prisoner from Pentonville.

He was sensitive to the public and private reception of his drawings. He had no cause to complain of the reviewers, nor did he; they were, I think, universally his admirers, nearly always expressing pleasure and relief that his invention and humour on the chosen musical theme were unfailing. With each new volume the size of edition and reprints mounted, and there would be frequent calls as publication day drew near to learn the latest figures, and to satisfy himself that stocks were adequate. I never felt that his interest was simply financial, his delight was

in the numbers for themselves and
in the proof that his humour
had not lost its touch.

During his last
few weeks, it seems to me that Gerard broke new
ground. He produced five drawings that are outstanding in their
various ways, and which are unlike anything he had done before.
There is a lovely painting of an old lady trombonist who has extended the slide of her trombone so far out that the frame of the
picture has to be carefully adapted in order to accommodate its
length. One day as we passed an antique shop in
Kensington Church Street, Gerard's attention
was suddenly arrested. There in the window
was a small harp-shaped mirror. It was about 18
inches high, its heavy brass frame ornately
decorated with cherubs and leaves. It seemed
very expensive at the time, but throwing caution
to the wind we bought it. At home the mirror was
quickly removed and replaced by a piece of clear
glass, behind which a few days later, sat the drawing of a splendid lady harpist plucking away at her
strings.

In much the same way a tambourine, its jingles
removed, served to represent a drum. Upon its vellum
Gerard drew a bass drum player; one hand holding his
stick, the other covering his mouth as he stares
disbelievingly at the large hole made in the vellum
by Gerard.

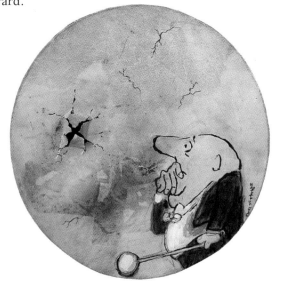

Five outstanding mus-
ical drawings which
Gerard produced in
his last few weeks,
Hoffnung in Harmony,
Souvenir Press ex-
cluding top right.

The other two paintings in this group were attempts to describe visually the sounds made by musical instruments, in one, the deep sombre notes of the double bass, and the contrast between the glittering high notes and the vibrant low notes of a harp in the other.

I use these drawings to form the focal points of the big Hoffnung Exhibition of original drawings. I practically never look at the brass harp without recalling with thankfulness our good judgement in deciding to purchase it that day in Kensington.

An idea that was not fulfilled was that of a soprano whose high note had shattered the glass in her frame. In order to achieve this Gerard intended placing a piece of clear glass over a shattered piece, which in turn would be secured from behind by the drawing of the soprano herself. Gerard's efforts to break the glass effectively were not successful. We were left with lots of broken glass and, alas, no end product – apart from a rough, pencilled sketch.

As if to counterbalance his exuberance and effervescence, Gerard was also a very serious person, keenly aware of the major issues of the day – racial prejudice, nuclear disarmament, homosexuality and prison reform. Donald Swann recalls:

To meet him then was a challenge. In our group of friends most were against apartheid and were prepared to say so. Gerard would suddenly appear on a platform speaking violently against it in public, or one would hear of his refusing to appear in South Africa before a segregated audience. Was it a good idea? Did we agree? It was a challenge. Quickly one had to say something. The same with prison reform. Before some of us had had time to study the first page of our circulars from the Howard League for Penal Reform, Gerard was an enrolled prison visitor, in the real heart of the action. I consider this a breakthrough from the vaguely thinking liberal into the active worker, the doer of the Word.

Closer to home he was sensitive to the needs of the deprived and underprivileged and troubled individuals struggling in situations Gerard saw as inhuman and unjust. All called for his help. He struck up friendships with the milkman, the postman, the dustmen, and on one particular occasion, with the rag-and-bone man. I never knew what chance remark sparked that get-together. I do remember returning home one morning to find a horse-and-cart tethered to the lamp post outside the house and the elderly owner sitting in Gerard's study listening to Stravinsky's Symphony in Three Movements, Gerard's latest piece recorded from the radio the previous evening. It was a curiously touching spectacle, Gerard wholeheartedly enthusiastic and intent on sharing his keen enjoyment of the music, the rag-and-bone man happily bemused, not, I think, from the effect of the music but by the welcome diversion that the day had provided.

Gerard's particular concern was prison reform, and after we married he became a prison visitor. In between the demands that work made on his time he regularly went off to Pentonville prison to visit some of the inmates there.

Visiting took place in the evenings, but other demands were sometimes made in the daytime. One of Gerard's men, who had been having problems with his wife, was anxious and worried as the time of his release approached. On the day, Gerard met him at the gates of Pentonville and drove him to his home in Hertfordshire. It was not such an exceptional thing to do, but I think it made all the difference. On the way they stopped to buy a small gift for the wife. When they arrived they all sat and talked over a cup of tea. Gerard cheered them and made them laugh a little easing the initial strain of the meeting, reassuring them and leaving them in an atmosphere of harmony and hope. He kept in touch with them and they later came to tea with their children.

Merfyn Turner, social worker and prison visitor, founder of Norman House, a home for discharged prisoners in north London, became, as did his wife, a much-respected friend of ours. He and Gerard first met at one of the quarterly meetings at Pentonville where the governor and prison visitors gathered to discuss their work. Merfyn writes:

New visitors were introduced to their fellow visitors, but 'Gerard Hoff-nung', the chairman said, 'needs no introduction.'

I doubt if anyone at the meeting that night fully anticipated the impact Gerard was to make on our quarterly meetings.

He was a fighter. Every visitor was given a book, in which the names and numbers of prisoners magically appeared. These were the men we visited. We were never told why they had been selected in the first place, nor how they had been allocated. Our job was to visit.

Gerard raised the matter at the first opportunity. 'I'm given a list of men to visit. I know nothing about them. I don't know why they're here, how often they have been here before, whether I'm to believe what they tell me or not. Mr. Chairman! Why can't we see the men's records?'

The meeting froze, as it always did when mention was made of prison records. 'Why can't we see the records, Mr. Chairman? I ask you, Why? Why? Why?' There were good reasons why prisoners' records were inaccessible to any except the privileged few. In any case, the secretary explained, the rules forbade it. Gerard exploded. 'Then for goodness sake, Mr. Chairman, why don't we change the rules?'

More social work was done immediately outside the prison gates in those days when visiting time was over, than was accomplished inside. We thought so, at least. 'We must do something,' Gerard insisted. 'The man is sick. He's out of his mind. He should never be in prison. He doesn't know what he's doing half the time. Nobody understands him. What can we do?' Then he would turn to me, and press me to promise to see the man. 'He's a fellow-countryman of yours, too,' he would add, as if that should settle all my doubts.

Alf was one of Gerard's men. He came to Norman House. He was unemployable, disorientated, schizophrenic; for twelve months we supported him until we were able to place him where he would be well cared for. But Alf disappeared, and was soon in prison again. For the next two years we kept in touch, mostly by letter. Alf's letters were phonetic, often unintelligible. But one message was always clear. 'Remember me to Hoffnung. Best friend I ever had.'

In prison, rumour has the quality of reality, but the rumour that swept the prison that Gerard Hoffnung was dead was indeed reality. For

29 SEP 1959

In replying to this letter, please write on the envelope:—

Number 9310 Name DENBY.
H.M. Prison, Pentonville,
Caledonian Road, LONDON, N.7. Prison

Dear Mrs Hoffnung

May I give you

my deepest simpathy for the lose

of your husband who was to

me the most sincure and

truest friend one could wish

to have I would like you

to know that I appreciate every

thing Gerard did for me and

I hope that one day I will be

able to show my appreciation

No. 243   (21442—3-11-42)

the men who had had the closest relationship with him, the shock was greater than they could absorb. 'I don't know what to think,' Stan said as he sat on his bed and looked at me as I sat where Gerard had so often sat before. 'When my own mother died, I didn't feel like this.'

Some days passed before Stan was able to tell me what Gerard's death meant to him. He had lost more than a visitor who had cheered him on countless visits, and helped him to forget the misery of his own loneliness. He had lost more than a friend. He had lost the only family to which he felt he really belonged.

'When blokes like me go to see people like Gerard, you expect them to take up the carpets. He had such a smashing home. But not him. He and his wife pulled me in. They cooked me a meal. They made me feel at home. They even let me play with their children. It was home to me.' He paused for a while.

'Do you know,' he said, 'I've done quite a bit of bird in my time. I always refused a prison visitor, until I got Gerard last time I was here. I thought I might as well try one. He changed things for me. He even made me want to go straight.'

'On my way to Meeting this morning, a little bird told me...'.

I received other letters from Gerard's men after his death; one reproduced here, expresses how much he meant to them.

For some time Gerard had been interested in the Religious Society of Friends – the Quakers. It was their deep-rooted concern for pacifism which first attracted him. He also sympathised with their concern for the individual, regardless of race, creed, nationality; their practical application of the Christian faith and their belief that all life is a sacrament.

He found the uncluttered form of worship, its quietness and simplicity, appropriate for him, and the remarkable potentiality of the silence helped further his quest for moral and spiritual meaning to our existence.

Twelve o'clock shuffle.

With no priest or choir or ritual, a Quaker Meeting depends for the richness of its experience on its members and Gerard, surely enriched the Meeting at Golders Green. Here is how Morag Morris remembered him:

He was, usually, one of the later arrivals . . . He would tiptoe stealthily across the floor to the far side of the Meeting House, compact in a tweed suit or in an ample pullover of cherubic blue or, once, in leather shorts, braced and brief in German fashion.

He would settle himself solemnly in one of the few armchairs, cross-legged, chin propped in cupped hand, frowning deeply. From time to time throughout the Meeting he would uncoil himself, to the minor discomfort of his neighbours (for which reason Annetta chose to sit far off) and knot himself up again, facing obliquely across the room. Or he would sit thoughtfully cracking his knuckles, one by one. In the main, though, he appeared sunk in contemplation, or attentive while some other member spoke.

Even in Meeting, though, Gerard's imagination was at work. He once told me it was there that some of the best ideas for his drawings came to him.

One Sunday, during the notices at the end of Meeting, Gerard read out a letter purporting to have come from a Temperance worker: an urgent request for an assistant to represent the evils of alcohol. The plea became more and more colourful and in the end turned out to be a giant leg-pull. Some were shocked, thinking it neither the time nor the place. But I do not know of any members who have not delighted in his endearing and tenderly de-bunking drawings on a Quaker theme.

The summer of 1959 came and went. We took the children to Folkestone for a few gloriously warm days leaving them with my parents while we drove to Cornwall. We had parted reluctantly with our little Austin 10 and felt better able to contemplate what to us then was a long journey! I remember two things about our stay in a hotel en route. One is the Abbey clock (possibly it was at Sherborne) which chimed quarter-hourly and disturbed us dreadfully. The other was the upset I caused when I inadvertently failed to notice that Gerard did not have a mous-tache. He had announced his decision to grow one a week or two previously and was fascinated by the ginger-tinged growth on his upper lip; the effect, though, was not to my liking and I quietly made my feelings known. Before we left our hotel I slipped out to buy a few things and on my return sensed an

uneasy atmosphere. The feeling persisted on the journey. What could this be? Had I done something? Said something? We had covered some distance before the penny dropped and I realised that the man sitting next to me was clean-shaven once more! Much later on, I found a photograph of Gerard on which he had been trying out the effect of a moustache.

In Cornwall we visited Malcolm Arnold and his wife Sheila. A deep friendship and understanding existed between Malcolm and Gerard and I like to think that they had those few happy days together.

We would have chosen to stay away longer but work drew Gerard back to London. It would never have occurred to us to be apart. Indeed, except for the times in hospital when our children were born and the rare occasion when one or other of us stayed overnight on a visit, we were never separated for more than a few hours.

Royal Festival Hall

General Manager : T. E. BEAN, C.B.E.

Monday, Sept 21 · 11 p.m.

A MIDNIGHT SHOW

In aid of the Campaign for Nuclear Disarmament

stars in our eyes

Including the following artists :

PEGGY ASHCROFT

JILL BALCON

BENJAMIN BRITTEN

CONSTANCE CUMMINGS

LEWIS CASSON

CECIL DAY-LEWIS

GERARD HOFFNUNG

DENIS MATTHEWS

JOHN NEVILLE

PETER PEARS

MICHAEL REDGRAVE

Compered by   **SYBIL THORNDIKE**

J. B. PRIESTLEY   **STANLEY UNWIN**

Looking in Gerard's diary I see he opened the Hampstead Garden Suburb Horticultural Show on 19 September 1959 and on 21 September took part in a late-night concert 'Stars in our Eyes' at the Royal Festival Hall in aid of CND. Gerard was by now thoroughly at home with this concert platform, for apart from his own productions he had more recently been soloist there in a performance of Vaughan Williams' Tuba Concerto with the Morley College Symphony Orchestra.

This time his tuba quartet performed a special arrangement by Wilfred Josephs (whose more recent compositions have become delightful additions to the Hoffnung Concert repertoire) of the Pizzicato from *Sylvia* by Delibes. Altogether, with the distinguished cast, it was a great occasion. Surrounded by his friends, working for a cause he believed in and playing his beloved tuba, this was surely, a most fitting finale.

A week later on 28 September Gerard died. At his funeral service it was said that he was the first professional jester Quakers had known in their 300 years. Gerard would have been pleased with this accolade.

myself (I think!)

POSTSCRIPT

A sense of loss at the sudden and unexpected death of an artist frequently brings a surge of interest in his work. Afterwards the name is often too soon forgotten. In Gerard's case, the public's refusal to let go was evident from the start and I soon became aware of this as a variety of events took place.

The memorial volume, *O Rare Hoffnung*, to which many friends contributed, and from which I have quoted liberally in this book, was brought out by Putnams. Its publication coincided with the first anniversary of Gerard's death and with the memorial concert held at the Royal Festival Hall. This event took the form of a Hoffnung concert, to which artists and musicians gifted time and talent and which was a hilarious and exuberant occasion.

While at the back of my mind I realised that I must find work and a regular income, I was frequently waylaid by other considerations. Decca brought out the record of Gerard's speech at the Oxford Union. It was an instant hit and has sold steadily since. Later, the Open University approached me with a strange request. They wanted to use the Bricklayer Story, perhaps the best loved of Gerard's anecdotes, to illustrate a technical point.

For BBC *Monitor* programme, Humphrey Burton made an enchanting short film from a selection of the drawings. The film, narrated by John Amis, was described by a critic as a brilliant exploitation of the camera's capacity to give static objects a dimension of music. This film never fails to give me pleasure.

Gerard's illustrations to Lady Pakenham's (Countess of Longford) articles, 'Points for Parents' became the small book, *Hoffnung's Little Ones*. Thumbnail drawings that had once illustrated book review columns, were collected and published as *Hoffnung's Constant Readers*. There followed *Birds, Bees and Storks*, depicting a

Work done equals force × distance (or potential energy gained).
Force equals mass × acceleration.

$$\text{Acceleration} = \frac{T' - 100g}{100} \text{m s}^{-2}$$

$$\text{or} = \frac{150g - T'}{150} \text{m s}^{-2}$$

$$T' = 120g \text{ N}.$$

$$\text{Work done} = 600g \text{ J}$$

$$a = \tfrac{1}{58}g \text{ m s}^{-2}.$$

Figure 4 '. . .the barrel of bricks was heavier than I was.'

father's embarrassment as he discusses the delicate subject with his son. The book *The Boy and the Magic*, written by Colette and translated by Christopher Fry, with Gerard's illustrations, was published in 1964. In between, *The Penguin Hoffnung* appeared, and later *Hoffnung's Encore*, which published for the first time, the Chelsea Arts Ball and the Glyndebourne designs, and many others. Each sold, with subsequent reprints.

All this work was time-consuming and I had little opportunity to search for a more solid occupation. Meanwhile musician friends, still reluctant to abandon the concerts, banded together to present The Hoffnung Astronautical Festival. Inspired by suggestions that Gerard had already shared with them, new ideas for this next venture were soon fast flowing.

On a night in February 1961, eight new works were premiered at the Royal Festival Hall and took their places in the repertoire. The critics were generous with their acclaim. Some wrote tongue-in-cheek, others more seriously. The *Financial Times* reported:

. . .*the best and most serious, and funniest piece in the programme was Lawrence Leonard's Mobile for Seven Orchestras . . . simply listening to large orchestras wandering all over the hall in a haphazard improvisation, and then assembling, both physically and musically, on to a tremendous unison, was an adventure for the ear. When this unison - to which 24 trumpeters added their voices - yielded to, of all things,* The Lost Chord, *the effect was surprising, ridiculous, and at the same time thrilling . . .*

For myself, I remember particularly how Sir William Walton teased the audience by conducting, after elaborate foreplay, a brief excerpt from *Belshazzar's Feast* – ending suddenly with the shouted word 'S L A I N !' echoing dramatically round the hall. It was a brief performance, but it brought the house down.

Despite the success of the evening, of the subsequent E M I disc and the wealth of goodwill and enthusiasm, the writing was on the wall. Two critics remarked, as most of us realised, that Gerard was sadly missed. Later, William Mann was quite frank:

It was impossible that a Hoffnung concert could work without Himself at the helm. The humour in the new works written for this last concert can raise smiles but the true Hoffnung quality, explosive, madly sane, irrepressible, is not there, could not be, alas. Concerts of comic music may well occur again. Hoffnung made them possible and popular, but there can be no Hoffnung without the

physical presence and continual imagination of Gerard. He was a once-off, humorist and dedicated musician. If someone so gifted in so many ways ever arrives on the scene again, I hope we will greet him with ninety times nine.

My children with Daniel Barenboim after he had opened the Hoffnung exhibition in Edinburgh.

However, the following year, Sir Ian Hunter, of Harold Holt Ltd, who had promoted most of the past concerts, sent a group of us, at the request of the Northern Sinfonia, up to Newcastle to perform four concerts in the north-east. The audience responded enthusiastically, but the experiment was not repeated.

Meanwhile, in 1964, I moved to a smaller house in nearby Hampstead; this has been my home and haven ever since. My children quickly settled happily in their new surroundings. It was a good move.

In the same year, Halas and Bachelor, in collaboration with the BBC, made a series of animated cartoon films, six of which were based on Gerard's musical cartoons. A further film, narrated by Peter Sellers, was based on *Birds, Bees and Storks*. I have always had reservations about these films, for I soon discovered that any form of adaption of the drawings inevitably altered drastically, their unique character. Further, the task of concocting six stories from the limited number of drawings was too much even for the most talented crew.

Despite this, the BBC have shown these films repeatedly. I derive little benefit however; owing to some unfortunate oversight in my contract with Halas and Bachelor and the BBC, I have earned from them over the years a total of £504.

Later in 1964 the Berlin Festival mounted the first big Hoffnung exhibition of original drawings. It attracted much attention and crowds streamed through the exhibition, smiling, chuckling, many laughing aloud, as they passed from one frame to another. This scene was repeated many times at home and abroad. Of the exhibition at

the Edinburgh Festival in 1968 *The Scotsman* commented:
Nothing can be more certain than everyone's enormous delight at the Festival exhibition so deservedly devoted to the endearing illustrations of that gentle clown of draughtsmen, Gerard Hoffnung. . . . there are 416 drawings, the verve of whose witty and often surreal invention is matched by a skilled linear simplification that demands their appraisal in the terms of fine art.

And *The Guardian* followed suit:
Never before at an Edinburgh exhibition can so many visitors have been heard giving way to uninhibited laughter as the crowds filing through the Hoffnung exhibition. . . . In all, this exhibition is guaranteed to keep you happy for as long as you have the time to spare.

The gradual deterioration in the condition of the drawings caused me anxiety. The constant framing and unframing and dispatching to various places made me increasingly aware of the risk of damage. Worse, one or two of them were lost.

'The lonely maharaja drank a glass of ink.'

It was the Welsh Arts Council who recognised this predicament and to whom I am endlessly grateful for their prompt, positive and generous action. They stepped in and, for the very small return of touring the exhibition in Wales, mounted, framed and crated the whole collection. Now nearly 500 drawings were safely behind perspex, residing handsomely in some four score large oak frames. These, in turn slotted into fifteen strong, felt-lined, wooden crates. The overall weight of the full crates made transportation costly and restricted journeys to Europe. This time it was the British Council who provided a solution, constructing a superb travelling exhibition of fine reproductions and enlargements.

While it was never intended to replace the display of originals, this exhibition has a quality of its own, magnifying as it often does, the intricacies and detail of Gerard's work. Light in weight, easily erected by people on the spot, posing few security problems, it has travelled world-wide and has visited scores of places the more cumbersome collection is less likely to reach – Yugoslavia, Rumania, Hungary, Turkey, Cyprus, Spain, the USA, Australia, New Zealand, India and Brazil – the list still grows.

My original three-year agreement with the British Council was twice renewed and still the exhibition seemed reluctant to return home. Eventually, after more than seven years of journeying from country to country, it arrived travel-worn and triumphant at a warehouse in north London, to become from now on my property and responsibility. Its crates were battered, but the contents were still in remarkably good condition. Now, after a period of rest and refurbishment, the exhibition is on the move again,

this time to lighten the hearts of customers at a large bank
in Switzerland!

Some years later I was contacted by Sheila Paine of London
University's Institute of Education. She had recently been impressed
by some drawings of Gerard's, done as a child, which I had shown in
an illustrated talk, and she wanted to reproduce one or two. Though
I told her I had many more to choose from, she was not prepared for
the feast that awaited her:

*I was astonished to discover how many of his early drawings had been
preserved. Even now when children's drawing is enjoying new interest, it
is rare to find continuous sequences from any one child, even in limited
numbers. Yet it is these sequences that are needed if we really want to
know how children's expressive and imaginative skills develop.*

Helped by the generosity of the Institute of Education and others,
Sheila designed 'Young Hoffnung', a chronological study of Gerard's
early development, mounting and framing 220 of the drawings and

Fright and Irascibility.
Drawn at the
age of seven years.

interspersing these with childhood photographs of Gerard, and explanatory text.

It has certainly not been easy to choose for display from so large a number of fascinating drawings. Initially my choices were governed by an intention to show, objectively, the many facets and stages of development in this one individual, rather than the person behind the drawings. But such objectivity has proved quite impossible, for the artist reveals himself constantly in the ideas expressed and in the manner of expression. I can no longer view the drawings other than with a sense of involvement in them and as an encounter with Gerard Hoffnung himself.

With advancing years, I am increasingly concerned that the original drawings contained in these two exhibitions remain intact and that a permanent home is found for their display, preferably in this country and ideally in London; for this was the city where Gerard was at home and where almost all his work was done. This display would be a real tonic for viewers and for this reason alone should not be discounted.

Meanwhile, the concerts refused to lie down. Despite the lull in the London performances, requests to use works from the concert repertoire regularly fell on my doormat. Some came from far afield, from Canada and the States, Australia and New Zealand and one from Tokyo. Most were from Europe and much time was spent on the wearisome task of packing and dispatching parcels of music to their various destinations. There were compensations – a trip to New York for a performance of the *Concerto Popolare* by the New York Philharmonic under Kostelanetz, with soloist Leonid Hambro, which accompanied a showing of Gerard's drawings at the Lincoln Centre. There was a highlight when I flew out with Peter Ustinov, who was presenting a concert which included Hoffnung works, at the Festival in La Rochelle. As the minute aircraft taxied down the runway it stopped and, at the pilot's request, Peter Ustinov and I were obliged to change places in order to balance the plane!

In 1968 a vast Hoffnung concert was held as a late night finale at the Edinburgh Festival. Here James Loughran was our conductor, the Amadeus Quartet our distinguished vacuum soloists. A visitor to the artists' entrance at the Usher Hall may have been under the impression that the concert was being held backstage, as members of the Scottish National Orchestra, twenty minutes behind schedule, collided as they came off the platform with players of the BBC Scottish Orchestra, who were waiting to take their places.

The Amadeus Quartet rehearse on floor polisher and vacuum cleaners.

When, in the early seventies, the London Music Club asked me to speak to their members about Gerard's life and work, I was not at all enthusiastic. The thought alarmed me, for I was unused to public speaking of any sort, and I was all the more disquieted when I realised that the challenge would have to be accepted. I did not even know how to begin the talk. Then a friend helped. 'Come round with pencil and paper and we'll get something written down.'

I can remember little about that first talk, except my unbounded relief when it was all over. It seems that it was a success. I was pleased with myself. Shortly afterwards came invitations from the Richmond Music Club and the Royal Philharmonic Society, and others followed. Gradually the talk evolved. My friend, Morag Morris, listening with a critical ear, made substantial improvements to it. Slides were amassed and a helpful friend at the BBC pieced together, on tape, various extracts from Gerard's recordings. I acquired my own film copy of *The Hoffnung Symphony Orchestra*.

Once I had organised all the material for my talks, I readily accepted invitations from Penzance to Aberdeen and almost everywhere in between. I found myself in Dublin and Belfast, on the Isles of Man and Arran, and to my amazement, speaking at the Oxford and Cambridge Unions, where I have returned on several occasions.

Dragging myself away from home was often a chore. Long drives could be tedious and tiring, but the audiences' reaction made it all worthwhile.

My memory is also enriched by a number of solitary and idyllic picnics on cliff-tops, aloft on some fell in Cumbria, or by some burn in Scotland, as I journeyed from one place to another.

And then, in 1976, I met Tom Bergman. We had met before, but only very briefly, during the early sixties in connection with some Hoffnung concerts performed in the north-east of England. Now he phoned to ask if he might promote such a concert in the Albert Hall in London. After even more frenetic activity than usual, including the preparation of a rare performance of *Let's Fake an Opera*, the event, true to form, was a great success.

But there was more to it than that. I found Tom's good humour, kindliness and wisdom a delight. I was surprised by the breadth of his activities and interests and soon discovered that his knowledge of music, his political acumen and his organizational abilities were remarkable. But, most important of all, he brought humour to every aspect of his life and he made me laugh.

It was a miracle to discover Tom. He became my close companion, co-director of the concerts and my guide and mentor in almost everything else. He was from a similar background to Gerard's. Both came from central Europe (Tom was born in Prague of Czech parentage), both were from well-to-do middle-class, Jewish families and both were refugees from Nazi persecution, having reached England in their early teens in 1939. Both were gourmets and, I am sorry to say, tended to be overweight.

It was Tom's idea to take the Hoffnung concerts abroad to those symphony orchestras eager to become involved in such a venture. Much careful preparation was to be made before we journeyed to our destination. Conductor, soloists, artists would be discussed and engaged, scores and parts, programme notes and publicity material despatched, lists drawn up of props required and other details confirmed. We would allow ourselves ten days at the venue for final

preparation and rehearsal before directing the performance.

In no time at all, or so it seemed to me, we were en route to Australia where, at the invitation of the Sydney Symphony Orchestra, we were to produce a concert in the Sydney Opera House. There we coached our bottle-players, ballerina, children's choir and others, amassed our props, rehearsed our conductor and soloists, searched out a street band, advised the hose-pipe player on the Thespian aspects of his performance, as well as the length and variety of hose-pipe required, conferred with lighting and sound technicians at the hall and settled endless details.

Television and radio interviews so enthused the public to hurry out to buy tickets for the performance that, on the night, the concert hall was filled to overflowing. The Australian Broadcasting Corporation televised the proceedings and the whole event was acclaimed. We felt vastly encouraged.

After that there was no let-up. We produced concerts in most parts of the world: in Helsinki, Oslo, Brussels, Frankfurt, Paris, Vienna, Zurich, Jerusalem and Copenhagen, in the Hollywood Bowl in Los Angeles, in Houston, Pasadena, Buffalo and Toronto and again in Australia and scores of other places. Sometimes we were asked whether there were ever difficulties with audience appreciation in the different countries we visited, but we never experienced any such problems. Cowboys in Montana, sophisticates in Los Angeles and even the very serious Finns have delighted in the subtleties of Hoffnung humour, as have the great (and the very definitely not so great) orchestras with whom we worked. In due course Tom undertook to conduct three of the pieces in the repertoire, thereby fulfilling one of his great ambitions.

Our prospects for 1992 looked particularly exciting. In February we presented a concert in the famous Gewandhaus in Leipzig, and in April came our first visit to Japan, where we toured three concerts alongside a grand showing of the exhibition. These were stirring events, but in no way did they compete with our third engagement of that year.

At this point I need to go back in time and to explain that, after serving in the RAF during the war, Tom had returned to Prague in 1946. The coup in 1948 forced him to escape again, at an hour's notice, across the border into Austria. He again found his way to England, which became his permanent home.

Until the political developments of the early nineties took place in Czechoslovakia, any return to that country had been out of the question. When we went in May 1992 to perform a Hoffnung concert in the Smetana Hall in Prague as part of the Prague Spring Festival, it was Tom's first visit to his homeland for 44 years; a heart-moving and thrilling experience for him and one in which I was very happy to be able to share. The concert was a fine success, not least Tom's address to the audience in Czech.

The tragedy came some ten days later when we were taking a brief holiday in Carlsbad. There he was admitted to hospital, where two days later he suffered a heart attack and died almost immediately. Amidst the dreadful turmoil and shock I was comforted and even rejoiced that he had, after so long an absence, been able to return to his homeland.

Now, more than a year later, my life is slowly beginning to take shape again and in the process some interesting things are happening. My son Benedict, a professional musician, is becoming more and more involved with the concerts and his help has already proved invaluable. I am very fortunate in having the dedicated support of Robin Ashby, Tom's friend and former business partner. His expertise is of paramount importance, for without his diligence and business skills we would indeed be in a sorry state. In organizing new concerts we are very fortunate in having wonderful soloists who are also our loyal friends.

My daughter Emily, a sculptor by profession, gives me constant help and support with the running of the exhibition, which has been on show for much of this year in London and other parts of the country.

We all miss Tom, his warmth and vigour and the laughter he inspired. Laughter is a great reliever of the misfortunes of life. Those who can generate it without hurt give pleasure and strength, and I am grateful to Gerard and Tom for that.

INDEX

An italic figure indicates an illustration